Attaining Maturity

By
LUELLA COLE

FARRAR & RINEHART, INC.
New York   Toronto

WAR EDITION

Complete text—reduced size
in accordance with paper conservation
orders of the War Production Board.

COPYRIGHT, 1944, BY LUELLA COLE LOWIE
PRINTED IN THE UNITED STATES OF AMERICA
BY THE FERRIS PRINTING COMPANY, NEW YORK
ALL RIGHTS RESERVED

*To
My Brother
A. H. C.*

Preface

THIS BOOK presents admittedly only one person's opinions. It is essentially a summary of my own observations of life and people during the first fifty years. Naturally, I have had to use my own experiences as a basis for what I have written, since they are the only ones I have ever had! If I occasionally seem dogmatic, that is only because my opinions happen to be rather definite and strong, not because I think I have had a unique revelation. I assume from the start that readers will have enough wit to weigh what they read and come to their own conclusions in the light of whatever experiences they have had. I have certainly tried to be exact and objective, but no one is omniscient.

Some of the readers who gave their judgment upon this book in manuscript felt that a disproportionate number of my illustrations were drawn from the life academic. Since all my descriptions of people are true stories, in spite of their careful camouflage, not fairy tales, I have had to take them where I have found them. The nub of the matter is that a disproportionate amount of my life has been spent in sundry halls of learning. Teachers are, however, not a race apart; what is true of them is equally true of nonteachers, since I do not deal with them in their instructional capacity but merely as human beings who have to face and solve the same situations in daily life as other people.

This book is not specifically about the war, although one section deals with problems of maturity as related to wartime conditions. It was, however, precipitated by the war, because the need for mature points of view is daily becoming more evident. Agreement with the particular things I have said about being a true adult is not as important as the careful consideration by each reader of what he thinks are the attributes of maturity. It is with the hope that it may provoke such discussion as will lead to more mature attitudes in these troubled times that the book has been written.

L. C.

November, 1943.

Contents

	PAGE
Preface	vii

PART I THE NEED FOR MATURITY

1. Mankind and the Modern World — 3
2. The Advantages and Disadvantages of Maturity — 10

PART II THE CRITERIA OF MATURITY

3. Intellectual Maturity — 21
4. Emotional Maturity — 40
5. Social Maturity — 53
6. Moral Maturity — 69

PART III POPULAR ESCAPES FROM MATURITY

7. Escape by Fantasy — 83
8. Escape by Play — 95
9. Escape by Solitude — 99
10. Escape by Fanaticism — 105
11. Escape by Projection — 114
12. Escape by Sophistication — 120
13. Escape by Illness — 126

CONTENTS

PAGE

PART IV SOLUTIONS FOR THE MATURE PERSON

14. Living with Yourself as You Are ... 135
15. Living with Others as They Are ... 145
16. Living in the World as It Is ... 155

PART V MATURITY AND THE WAR

17. Mature Attitudes in War and Peace ... 161

PART I

The Need for Maturity

CHAPTER I

Mankind and the Modern World

HUMANITY is too bright for its own good. It has created a world to which it seems unable to adjust adequately. Human ingenuity and human persistence have produced a world civilization that has turned into a Frankenstein (monster) and gone out of control; global culture and life have been replaced by global war and death. Even the modern life of peacetime does not appear to be an environment to which man can readily adapt himself. On the one hand he is overprotected physically, while on the other he is underprotected emotionally. His technological progress has removed many a simple problem of existence, but it has precipitated a whole new set of difficulties of so severe a nature that many an individual has been overwhelmed by them.

Within recent times people have had more opportunity than ever before to live childish lives because of the protection given them by their modern, mechanized environment. Most practical problems of daily life are solved for them; to get water one turns a faucet, to get heat one sets a thermostat, to get light one punches a button. Throughout the day's work one goes from gadget to gadget. Such protection of the physical man encourages a prolongation of childishness and dependency. Primitive life gave no such protection, and frontier life was almost equally stern. If the processes of merely existing become exacting enough, they take the childishness even out of children, and conversely if they are made sufficiently simple they provide a milieu in which certain stimuli to maturity are lacking. Modern life, especially in periods of peace and prosperity, has a tendency to prolong childish attitudes and adolescent whims. The middle-aged women with not enough to do to keep them busy and not enough maturity to find contentment for themselves are the mainstay, not only of beauty parlors and freak religions but also of mental clinics. The middle-aged men who cannot hold a job because they react to strain in the manner of small boys swell the ranks of the spongers and the unemployed. A more primitive life would educate the educable and eliminate the others. Modern life, because it gives adequate protection even for nitwits, has made possible a prolongation of childish behavior in many an individual.

From a social point of view, however, modern life is enormously complex and makes great demands upon man's powers of adjustment. From what science has learned about human beings it appears that they were never designed for living in a complicated environment. In fact, some psychologists have felt that mankind in general is incapable of understanding modern problems, of facing them, or of adjusting to them. Our technical progress has far outstripped our adaptability and has produced a world in which we cannot relax; we must constantly live beyond our social and emotional means, we must always be under too much pressure, and we must from time to time go through a period of exhaustion, bankruptcy, and regression while we recuperate. Such at least is the somewhat depressing opinion of many psychiatrists.

Engineers can build a tunnel under a river, can ventilate it, and can make it so safe that injury to life and limb is improbable, but they cannot so re-educate humanity that it has no misapprehensions about traveling through a hole in the ground, nor can they eliminate the nervous strain arising from vibration and noise. Similarly, men can build skyscrapers and elevators, but they cannot build a new human race that lives in them as naturally as fishes live in water. Let a train happen to stop in a tube, or an elevator stick between the twenty-eighth and twenty-ninth floors, and the surface adjustment soon gives way to primitive, unreasoning panic. In our intellectual, social, and economic milieu there are numerous sources of strain and discontent. Thus a man may spend the major part of his working life making castings, without knowing what becomes of them or how his work fits into the total economy. The teachers in the training school he attended probably taught him the necessary skills in a relatively short time, but it is unlikely that they included in their teaching a philosophy of life that would permit their one-time pupil to bear without strain the monotony of an existence devoted to making castings. Social patterns are as complex as those in the economic world. Modern life herds people together in thousands, but it does not give them the social skills they need to get along with each other. The airplane and the radio have combined to bring all countries in the world closer together, but technical development has not automatically produced sympathy among nations. We do not necessarily have more understanding of, more tolerance of, or more respect for the people of Norway, for instance, because we can now reach them in one day instead of ten, or can hear a broadcast in Norwegian, which we do not understand. In many instances education has not kept pace with invention, and mankind has acquired highly efficient and highly dangerous tools before it has been taught to use them properly and safely. Human beings do not seem to have the native capacities for an easy and automatic adaptation to the complex life of today, and it remains to be seen whether or not they can be educated into becoming more adjustable.

If people are protected too much they fail to emerge from childhood, and if they are protected too little they regress from their adult level and become children again. In the decade between 1920 and 1930, many a young American found life so easy and so full of fun that he never grew up at all. In the same period many a young German found life so impossibly difficult that he was willing to forsake what maturity he had gained and regress to a childish level. If one cannot meet life by himself he may cling to some person who is stronger and seems to have a solution for his difficulties. Failing to find such a person the regresser may fall back upon some private organization, the church, or the state. In daily life one sees numerous examples of this process of regression. For instance, there are those college graduates who continue for years to write their former professors asking for advice in this or that emergency; such dependence upon the teaching staff was once legitimate, but it is not supposed to continue throughout life. The young business man who discusses his work in detail with his superior or with his retired uncle is similarly immature. The man who, in times of peace, returns to the army for one enlistment after another, with intervals of trying other things in between, is usually glad to get back into a situation in which others tell him what to do. The nun and the monk turn their lives over to the church; it has been said that when a man decides to become a Jesuit he has made the last decision he will ever make.

In ordinary times there are always some individuals who regress because they cannot adjust to modern complexities. In times of stress, however, whole groups or even whole nations may revert to psychological infantilism and dependence in order to gain security. In the early history of Sparta, for instance, the Spartans were threatened with extinction or at least absorption unless they held together; their solution for the problem was to train boys and girls from childhood to take their places as members of the state. Education, food, clothing, and living quarters were all regimented, with the sole purpose of benefit to the state. At intervals ever since, whenever existence has become perilous, men have given up liberty in return for security. For instance, in the Middle Ages a man traded his personal freedom for protection. Just such a regression has taken place during the last twenty years in Germany. After their defeat in 1918 the Germans were disappointed, exhausted, discouraged, and half-starved; as time went on and things got worse rather than better, they became more and more bewildered, frightened, apprehensive, insecure, and discontented. They could not cope with life as free individuals, but a regression to a simpler level was still possible. Hence the totalitarian state came into being. There the individual is nothing, and the future of the state is everything; the citizen must not think for himself but must believe with his whole heart and soul what he is taught. The point that many Americans seem to overlook is that this regimentation is one of the possible solutions to the problem of adjustment to an overcomplex environment. It may not be the solution that you or I would care for, but it does remove the pressure from the individual. The state becomes his father and looks after him from the cradle to the grave, provided he will remain a submissive child and give to the state his devotion and trust. Nazism is therefore an answer to life's complexities, a solution by regression.

The American way of life requires a quite different answer—a solution by maturity. Such a solution assumes that the human animal is capable of learning how to control himself as well as he can control the forces of nature, that he can find within himself the power to adjust to the complex world he has created, that his emotional and social development can catch up with his intellectual achievements. If, then, the solution by individual, responsible maturity with its accompanying personal freedom is preferable to a solution by group regression with its regimentation and personal submission, it becomes necessary to consider of what maturity consists, how it may be reached, what tendencies may prevent its realization, and what its bearing is upon the present global confusion. To be effective, such thinking must be done by a large proportion of the world's population before mankind annihilates itself by means of its own inventions.

CHAPTER 2

The Advantages and Disadvantages of Maturity

IF A COMPETENT engineer had designed the world, he might have simplified the process of growing up by arranging for an orderly succession of habits and attitudes as an individual passed through one stage of growth after another. Thus the baby would automatically lose his babyishness when he became a child, his childishness when he became an adolescent, and his adolescent traits when he became an adult. Unfortunately *le bon Dieu* did not see fit to create such a psychological Utopia. To be sure, organisms lower than man do automatically shed one set of habits and substitute another; the caterpillar crawls, the pupa sleeps, and the moth flies about seeking fur coats to lay eggs in. These simpler organisms never get confused or carry into the next stage the habits appropriate to a preceding level. Mankind is not so lucky. Most of us enter our adult years burdened with immaturities of various kinds. To these we cling persistently until they are knocked out of us by adversity, and sometimes we do not have sense enough to abandon them even then. Human beings appear to have some choice in the matter and may grow up or not as they prefer. Some of them obviously do not prefer. Because people have a flexibility that is denied the lower animals, they can become what the psychologist calls maladjusted, a well-worn word which is polite lingo for sheer human idiocy. There are no maladjusted caterpillars, bees, or ants, although domesticated animals can become neurotic if their environment is sufficiently artificial. In the main, however, only mankind has the dubious honor of having enough mentality to be a fool.

Since human beings have some choice in the matter of growing up they should know what are the advantages and disadvantages of being an adult. The chief advantage is that one is as free as it is humanly possible to be. Children are always in bondage to their incapacities, their fears, their ignorance, their misconceptions, their emotions, and their immediate desires. Adolescents are somewhat freer in so far as their physical environment is concerned, but they are deeply dependent upon each other in social matters and upon the objects of their hero-worship for guidance in formulating their attitudes. This social bondage is fairly rigid; they all want to dress alike, to use the same catchwords, to do the same things, to have the same enthusiasms, to see the same movies—and woe betide the boy or girl who cannot or will not conform. Only an adult is able to be free, because at earlier levels he is too dependent upon others to establish true liberty for himself. This point will become clearer as the discussion continues.

A second advantage of maturity is that an adult finds contentment because he has learned to accept life as it is and his place in it. A child does not know enough about the world to be content except in the proximity of understanding adults who simplify his environment for him and help him to be happy. Adolescents are better equipped intellectually to face the world, but their ambitions are usually quite beyond their capacities. They want to enter social groups above their own, they want clothes they cannot afford, they want new and expensive cars, they want to enter the most difficult professions, they want to reform the world, they want excitement and thrills, they want to fall in love with a handsome hero or beautiful heroine, and so on. They do not have much contentment even though they may have excitement a-plenty, because their demands upon life usually exceed their supply of talents. Those individuals who grow up emotionally and socially make some kind of a compromise that permits them to be content.

Finally, an adult feels secure. Children have security only if their environment is so arranged as to give it to them; adolescents have greater physical security than children, but most of them are acutely aware of social, intellectual, or financial inadequacies. An adult has learned to adjust his work and play to his capacities, he has developed some understanding of life and of his place in it, and in general he has the feeling that he is the master of his fate. Intellectually, of course, he may realize clearly enough that his future depends upon a number of factors over which he has no control, but in his emotional tone he is not a prey to doubt, because he is quite sure he can solve difficulties in the future as he has solved those in the past. His basic sense of competence fortifies him against most childish or adolescent fears.

On the other hand being an adult has some drawbacks. For instance an individual must take the consequences, good or bad, of his own behavior. A child can sidestep consequences because he is not old enough to be responsible for them. An adult is. I admit that the necessity for facing consequences sometimes makes one wish to be a child again and let mother and father make apologies, pay off debts, promote social contacts, or decide vexing problems. The adult is strictly on his own. It is his privilege to carve out the kind of life he wants if he can, but since he expects to profit by his successes he must also be prepared to take the blame for his failures.

A second disadvantage of maturity is that one must walk alone, accompanied by loved ones to be sure, but essentially alone in an indifferent world. A child belongs to his family and friends, and he has not yet discovered that the world beyond his home does not and will not revolve around him. An adolescent generally begins to suspect that he is not the exact center of the universe, and bitterly he resents it. An adult has accepted the inevitable and knows that he is a mere speck of matter suspended in a second of time, and he does not fear the loneliness of his position—at least not often!

Being an adult is dangerous, but less dangerous than not being one. Maturity requires courage, lots of it, because one has to meet emergencies and solve them, instead of avoiding them and escaping into a fool's paradise of pretense. Mature people can endure strain without breaking under it only because they have courage. They do not get caught in the vicious circles that ensnare the coward. For instance, if a person attempts some task with an inner fear of failure, he is not likely to be successful on account of the tension to which his fear subjects him; his failure makes him more uncertain of himself than before and lowers his chances of succeeding in his next task. Thus he eventually develops a habit of failure that he cannot ever overcome. Or a student lacks the courage to attempt independent thought and relies upon his memory of what was in the books he has read, because remembering takes less courage than thinking; but the more material he learns by heart, the less able he is to think. He therefore gets into the vicious circle that ultimately produces the yes-man, the imitator, and the pedant. If an adult lacks courage, one of the numerous mental traps that lie in wait for the coward will almost certainly close upon him.

Probably no one is wholly mature. Most of us certainly retain one or more childish traits, even though we may be quite well aware that they are childish. One person stamps his foot when he is angry, another pushes himself into the conversation as a means of attracting attention to himself, a third is desperately afraid of thunderstorms, while a fourth falls in love with people twice his age, and a fifth cannot accept even the kindliest word of criticism without crying. Sometimes these childish traits

ADVANTAGES AND DISADVANTAGES

are right on the surface where they shine forth like beacon lights and sometimes they pop out only under pressure; in some cases they are simple and obvious, while in others they are submerged and devious. In these survivals each man carries around within him the child he once was. And from that child he will never completely escape. Hence the great importance of the early years.

In speaking of adults, then, I mean those who make mature responses most of the time, not paragons who never slip back into immaturity. If one were to judge himself or his friends by the criteria of maturity set forth in this or another book on the same topic, he would find that neither he nor they measured up to every specification. Certainly the portrait of the true adult as I have drawn it accords only moderately with my conception of myself or of my friends, most of whom nevertheless strike me as being indubitably adult.

In recent decades the relatively new science of child psychology has brought the importance of childhood home to parents and teachers, and rightly so, because it is the period during which the fundamental patterns of reaction are determined. The tendency has been, however, to neglect the preparatory function of childhood and to treat children as if they would never be anything else. Since psychologists and educators have already hammered into the public mind the paramount importance of childhood for its own sake, it might be well to look through the other end of the telescope for a while and to consider the years before adulthood as a period of preparation in the art of living. Because of the emphasis upon children and adolescents, the years of maturity have been neglected, in spite of the fact that a person who lives out his allotted three score years and ten spends the major part of his earthly existence as an adult. For such a person adulthood is twenty-five times as long as infancy (ages 1 and 2),* five times as long as childhood (ages 3 through 12), over six times as long as adolescence (ages 13 through 20), and two and a half times as long as all three put together. The pre-adult levels are important, not in themselves, but in their profound effect upon the adult they produce. That is, childhood could be important in and of itself only if children continued indefinitely to be children.

Even such dull reading matter as the census yields information about the importance of the adult years in comparison with those that precede them. In the latest census there were more than one and a half as many people over twenty as under. Moreover, this proportion is steadily becoming larger, as may be seen by a comparison of census returns for previous decades, of estimates of population for the years before the official census was taken, and of estimates for the future. In 1820 just half the population was below 16 years of age; those above 20 made up about forty per cent of the total. In 1860 this percentage had risen to fifty and by 1900 to fifty-six. At the present time, the average age of the population is 28 and the percentage of those above

* These and the following ages are only approximations.

20 has now become sixty-eight. In other words, the United States has emerged from its adolescence and has entered its national middle age. If present trends continue, by 1980 children and adolescents will be in a greater minority than they are now, and the expected per cent of adults in the population will be approximately seventy-five. In our own country at least, the world is already an adult world and as time rolls on it will presumably become even more so. An evaluation of adulthood is therefore distinctly appropriate. The years from twenty to sixty are not any too well understood; perhaps when they are better known we shall all be inclined to sing with the poet:

> Grow old along with me!
> The best is yet to be,
> The last of life, for which the first was made:
> Our times are in his hand
> Who saith "A whole I planned,
> Youth shows but half; trust God: see all, nor be afraid!"

PART II

The Criteria of Maturity

CHAPTER 3

Intellectual Maturity

EVERYONE develops mentally as he grows older, unless his nervous system suffers from injury, serious disease, or extreme deprivation. There is also considerable evidence that one's limits for mental growth are fixed by heredity, and that an average environment will provide the stimuli necessary for attaining one's adult mental stature. It is not then with general mental growth that this chapter has to deal but with the development of mature intellectual attitudes. The damsel of twenty-five who goes into a store to buy a grey suit and comes out with a bright green silk dress may have an adult mental age but she does not have adult habits of thought. Nature and environment may be trusted to develop intellectual capacities, but it takes education and training to use these capacities as an adult uses them.

Other people may select other criteria of intellectual maturity, but to me the grown-up person shows six characteristic habits of thought: he can make up his own mind, he can take responsibility, he can think objectively about himself and his work, he can maintain an open mind, he can make a workable compromise with life, and he can bear the indifference of the world to his own fate. Some of these statements may strike the reader as commonplace, but they are no more banal than life itself. To clarify what is involved, I am going to illustrate my points with examples drawn from among the acquaintances of fifty years in fully twenty places. These examples are, however, so completely camouflaged that a reader who thinks he can identify anyone is certain to be mistaken.

First, as to making up one's mind. There are lots of ways of doing it, and lots of reasons why people have trouble in the process. Only the fanatic, who is not without many other difficulties in adjusting to life, can make up his mind instantly about almost anything, even though his conclusions sometimes seem preposterous to you and me. And why is the fanatic so singularly blessed? Because he sees only one side of a question, he has an emotional tolerance for only one side, and he is so much under the dominance of a controlling concept that only one side interests him. Consequently, his decisions are in effect made for him. More normal people see the advantages and disadvantages of various possible courses of action, various motives urge them in one direction or another, and various interests have equally strong appeals. As a result, decision is difficult. The more definite one's preconceived ideas are, the easier is each successive decision; and, conversely, the man with an open mind may have a hard time coming to any decision at all. Although some people have intrinsically more difficulty than others in making up their minds, an adult succeeds in doing so, whether the process be hard or easy.

INTELLECTUAL MATURITY 23

From time to time I visit a family that has raised indecision to an art. The discussions generally start just before dinner and go on intermittently for two or three hours, the problem being who is to do what during the evening. If one member of the family has a definite engagement at a definite hour, he or she is greatly relieved to be well out of the daily wrangle. In the course of two hours I have heard the following plans promulgated for the disposition of the six people involved:

1. A, B, and C would go to a movie, D and E would play chess, and F would go to bed with a good book.
2. B, C, and D would go to a friend's house, A, E, and F would go skating.
3. C, E, and F would go to a show, A would do some work, B would study, and D would mend her socks.
4. A and C would go to see one movie, B and F another, and D and E a third, all parties meeting at a café later.
5. A, B, D, and E would dance at a night club, C and F would just stay home.
6. Everyone would remain at home and several guests would be asked to come in and play cards.
7. B and E would go swimming, A would get his third typhoid shot at his doctor's, C and D would make a visit to Chinatown, and F would do anacrostics at home.

This type of discussion goes on almost every evening and is generally settled by the limitation of time. As the hands move around the clock, one possible line of action after another is closed because the hour has become too late. In the end the members of the group usually disperse about the house, amusing themselves with victrola, radio, card games, study, reading, and letter-writing. In more important matters this family shows a similar ineptitude about making up its mind. Vacation plans remain hazy until the days of freedom are half over, the question of what school Mary Jane shall attend next year drags on until the opening day of school forces a decision; planning the daily menu may literally take over an hour, and the process of getting any member of the group into a hospital for a needed operation requires a combination of brute force and grand strategy. On a national scale, the well-known technique of muddling through indicates much the same type of mental immaturity.

Because he can make up his own mind, an adult is not dependent upon authority. He may, and often does, consult other people but he does not follow their advice blindly, nor do they form his opinions for him as parents form a child's opinions. He respects tradition and takes it into account but he does not lean upon it. Occasionally one meets an adult who shows a marked inability to escape from the intellectual domination of his early years into the balanced judgment of maturity. Such a person was one acquaintance of mine.*

Miss T is a teacher of high school mathematics. She is relatively popular among both students and colleagues. It is admitted that she is not an especially stimulating person, and students tend to speak of her pleasantness and sympathy rather than of her instruction. She is the teacher to whom pupils go when they are in trouble. On Sunday afternoon she has "open house" where many pupils from her current classes gather, as well as several who were in her classes formerly. Socially she is unusually well adjusted and seems thoroughly content with her life and work. Other teachers like her so well that they show no jealousy of her popularity with the pupils. Of late years, however,

* Some of the individual histories in this book are taken from various books of mine, others are adaptations from the same sources, and still others are new. I refuse to bore either myself or a reader by giving page references. So I thereby give myself permission to quote myself when I feel like it. I assume the reader will not want the references anyway, since my previous productions are all textbooks and dull.

INTELLECTUAL MATURITY

the boys and girls have begun to speak rather slightingly of her teaching; they call her a "nice old thing," pay attention courteously in class, but are inclined to regard the time they spend there as largely wasted. When Miss T began to teach, the high school required that each student take a year of algebra. Miss T was in her element when explaining the mathematically obvious to a dull pupil. At the present time the requirement is no longer in force, and only pupils who like mathematics elect algebra. For those students Miss T is not a good teacher, and it is they who criticize her. An examination of her methods reveals the reasons for their attitude. She uses the same textbook that she herself studied in her high school days, although the school has changed texts several times and she is supposed to be using a more modern book. Of course she knows the problems by heart. She plods through the book each semester, point by point, varying her performance from year to year not at all. Her manner in class is charming, but she provides the superior pupils whom she now teaches with only meager intellectual stimulation. The trouble with Miss T does not seem to be a deficiency in native ability but rather a childish dependence upon authority. She clearly does not feel secure with any text except the one she has practically memorized. When pupils ask questions that are outside the scope of her one book, she answers them pleasantly enough but in effect brushes the queries aside and goes on as before. In faculty meetings Miss T expresses herself as though she were in favor of modern methods and she is indeed a progressive teacher as far as her personal relations with her students are concerned, but she resists innovations that would force her into intellectual independence. She is socially an adult, but her mental life is still in the childish level of dependence upon authority.

This woman showed her immaturity by her dependence upon what she regarded as the one true light within her field of knowledge. This type of behavior is different from the state of indecision described in the previous study, but it springs from a similar refusal to make independent decisions.

A true adult accepts the responsibility for his actions—a performance that requires intellectual maturity, because he must first see that results come from causes. The woman who complains that her husband no longer loves her as he did might well consider what causes have operated to produce this result. It may be that he never cared for her in the first place, or that he was a trifler, or that he now prefers someone else. Or it may be that she has caused his defection by letting him do the housework, by spending more money than he could make, or by failing to effect the fifty per cent of the marital adjustment that might reasonably be expected of her. There are few things more childish than the inability to see what produces what, or the unwillingness to apply one's knowledge of causation to one's own behavior. The three people described below illustrate various ways of rejecting responsibility.

In a rooming house there was one girl—Annie by name—who was discovered one afternoon drinking coffee with a boy friend in her room, with the door closed. It was improbable that she had done anything wrong, but having a man in her room was against the rules. The girl was given a warning by the landlady and was told that a repetition of the offense would mean immediate expulsion from the house. A week later Annie repeated the performance. The landlady ordered her to be out of the house within twenty-four hours, and would pay no attention to the tears and promises that followed. Annie had been fairly warned, and now she could take the consequences of breaking the rules. In a few hours Annie's mother arrived upon the scene and begged for a special dispensation that would permit her child to escape the results of the behavior. Throughout the next day the mother followed the landlady about, crying and imploring for "one more chance" for Annie, but without success. For the first time in the girl's life, her mother could not interfere between cause and effect. Annie had slid out of consequences because her mother had protected her from them. As a result she was childish, uninhibited, and silly. She spent the next few weeks in a small, dingy room, away from her friends, and learned for the first time that causes have results.

Dr. Franklin is a woman professor nearly forty years old. During her undergraduate days she seemed in general a normal person, although she showed even then a tendency to become irresponsible if work were uninteresting or too difficult, and to impose upon her friends. She had two or three serious arguments with her teachers and on one occasion had to be moved from one section to another because she and the teacher had become so profoundly antagonistic. She participated freely in nonacademic activities but, while efficient, she did not command much confidence from her associates because they sensed her irresponsibility. She was a member of several class athletic teams. On some days she would play well and on other days poorly, but she always resented being taken out of a game even though she knew she was playing badly. She knew she was supposed to retire early the night before a class game but she would often stay up late, either because she became interested in her work or from sheer negative suggestibility; as a result she would play poorly the next day. In spite of several such experiences she did not learn to go to bed on time or to submit to other training rules.

After leaving college she took graduate work and became an instructor of history in a small college. This position she held for two years but was then asked to resign. Three reasons were given: first, she was irregular about meeting her classes; if she were interested in doing something else she would simply cut class. Second, her teaching was often careless; her presentation was sure to be poor if she happened not to feel like teaching. Finally, she had developed several intense feuds with members of the faculty and administrative officers. Anyone who criticized her became at once her enemy. She constantly justified her absences from class and her poor teaching by complaining about the "inferior students"; actually, the students were above average in ability and preparation. At other times she would complain of overwork, absence of academic freedom, or lack of sympathetic understanding.

After losing her first job she obtained a position as assistant in a research project being carried on by a national foundation. Here she had the same difficulties. She accused her superiors of prejudice against her, of unnecessary criticism, and of overworking her. She was so generally unsatisfactory that when she handed in a careless and inaccurate report of certain funds she had had charge of expending, this matter was made an excuse for eliminating her.

For over a year Miss Franklin had no job. Eventually, however, she was offered a chance to take over the contract of a former friend for the duration of the academic year, with the understanding that her appointment would be renewed in case she was satisfactory. In spite of knowing she was on probation, Miss Franklin again neglected her classes and antagonized people. This particular position paid a much larger salary than any she had ever had, but instead of saving the money, she spent it on excursions to various large cities where she remained for several days and naturally failed to meet her classes. By the end of the year she realized she would not be reappointed, became very indignant, and left without ever turning in the grades for her courses. In spite of urgent requests she flatly

ATTAINING MATURITY

Books by Luella Cole

PSYCHOLOGY OF THE ELEMENTARY SCHOOL SUBJECTS

THE IMPROVEMENT OF READING

TEACHING IN THE ELEMENTARY SCHOOL

THE BACKGROUND FOR COLLEGE TEACHING

PSYCHOLOGY OF ADOLESCENCE

ATTAINING MATURITY

INTELLECTUAL MATURITY

refused to turn in her report. Finally, the college sent a personal messenger, who discussed the students' work with her and succeeded in getting from her some verbal statement of each student's standing. But even this information was difficult to obtain because of her constant complaints about the poorness of the student material, the inadequacy of the library, and the lack of academic freedom.

There next intervened four or five years during which her only employment was writing book reviews, typing theses, tutoring, doing minor research jobs or library work for other people. During this time she became permanently embittered and turned to communism and other forms of propaganda as outlets for her emotional attitudes. One of her more objectionable traits became emphasized; she "sponged" constantly on every acquaintance for meals, transportation, cigarettes, books, shows, and other things. There were several people who would willingly have supplied her with such things if she had not tried so obviously to get them for nothing. In spite of her serious characteriological defects, she was an intelligent and stimulating conversationalist. For an evening's entertainment one could hardly have a more charming guest. For short periods of time and in a congenial atmosphere none of her outstanding defects appeared at all. But she always defeated her own ends by her grasping attitude.

Through the combined efforts of several friends, Miss Franklin finally obtained a summer school position in a normal school. Here she repeated the identical tactics which had led to her dismissal from three previous positions. At the end of the appointment, she was again out of a job. During the following years she succeeded in supporting herself, rather precariously to be sure, with odd jobs, but with the beginning of the depression she became completely destitute. For years before the war she was on the relief rolls, and is now regarded as a totally unemployable individual, in spite of her high level of education and very real intellectual capacity.

Pedro was a handsome young Portuguese. His parents were literate, but neither had had much formal schooling. Pedro had a good mind and an especial talent for laboratory science. He had agreeable manners, spoke English with an intriguing accent, and had made a place for himself in the society of his peers. To earn money Pedro tended the gardens in a wealthy part of town. This work brought him in contact with many people of the upper social classes. One day Esther, the only child of a wealthy banker, saw Pedro in the garden, talked with him, and fell in love with him. Her parents were furious about the affair and threatened to disown her if she married him, but they had always been indulgent parents and had brought Esther up on the notion that she could have anything she asked for. Her whims had always been satisfied and she had experienced no difficulty in wrapping her parents around her little finger. Esther's father and mother tried to send her away on a trip around the world, but she eluded their vigilance and eloped with Pedro. Her parents have never spoken to Pedro and will not allow him in their house. They gave their daughter no financial aid when her babies were born, and she has had three children at home without a doctor and with only Pedro's mother to help her. In spite of poverty at first and of their different backgrounds, Esther and Pedro are still happy after ten years of married life. She is prematurely old because of hardships that could have been greatly lessened if her parents had been willing to accept her marriage. And there is no indication that they consider themselves in any way to blame. They continue their own lives as if nothing had happened. Esther may visit them whenever she wishes, but she may not bring either husband or children with her. They often invite her to the house to meet her girlhood friends. Always the talk flows on in amiable fashion, but it is restricted to matters that once concerned Esther although they are of no great moment to her any longer. She maintains the relationship partly because she hopes they may remember her in their

INTELLECTUAL MATURITY

wills. Esther's mother often gives her pretty and expensive dresses that Esther has no occasion to wear except on the rare formal dinners with her parents, but neither parent will loan her even a cent to buy Pedro a raincoat or to pay for having the baby's tonsils removed. In fact, if Esther mentions such matters, all graciousness disappears from her parents' behavior, and they stiffly leave the room in complete silence. For them Pedro and the children simply do not exist. They have made it unmistakably clear that the responsibility for the débâcle in their lives is all hers and that she may return home, alone, whenever she tires of poverty. To them she is not a well-balanced adult but a misguided child who has been led astray by Pedro's flashing smile. They give every evidence of expecting any moment that she will walk in and resume her former life as if nothing had happened.

The girl in the first story expected to be protected from consequences, the professor in the second refused to admit responsibility and blamed others, while the parents in the third preferred to bury their heads in the sand and make believe no results existed.

Taking responsibility seems to be extraordinarily hard for many people, if one can judge from the common inability or unwillingness to say either, "I don't know," or, "I was wrong." The human mind will seek the most elaborate excuses rather than admit ignorance or error. Whenever a person makes either of these remarks, he is openly accepting responsibility for himself, for his stupidity and his mistakes. Those who can say neither are still immature.

Few people can be wholly objective about themselves, but adults can succeed to some extent. They can evaluate their strength and their weakness, if they can only rid themselves of the illusion that what they do, think, and feel must be right because the acts, thoughts and feelings are their own. Human beings have a deep-seated tendency to misjudge the work of their own minds and hands. I suppose most of us have been called upon at some time or another to admire badly made place cards, banal music poorly executed, poorly baked cake, inane poems, or absurd gadgets, into which the creator has put his libido, on the principle that a sufficiently earnest desire will compensate for lack of skill. With a child this may be so, because one can hardly expect him to be objective. Little Johnny loves the boat he made merely because he made it, and its habit of promptly rolling over when put in water does not detract from its soul-satisfying beauty. With age one should become more objective about one's abilities and more critical of one's actions, but some people emphatically do not.

Mr. J is a charming young man of twenty-four. He is good-looking in a rather boyish way and has pleasant manners, especially toward older people. He has been earning his own living, mostly in dead-end occupations, since he was seventeen. He has plenty of ambition but attaches his enthusiasm to quite unreachable goals. At seventeen he decided to become a singer, left school and got a small job that allowed him some hours free each day for practice. For two years he worked hard and faithfully, but he simply did not have the necessary native talents to succeed. Thus far the story is not remarkable. Most adolescents have one or more episodes of this sort. Upon being disil-

INTELLECTUAL MATURITY

lusioned about his voice, Mr. J took up ballet dancing, although friends told him he was already much to old. Again he plunged into training, working at a job only enough to support himself and spending the rest of his time in training. For two years he was heart and soul for the ballet. He made some progress, but not enough to meet competition in an overcrowded market. He next became fascinated by radio work. He got a job as messenger boy in a large broadcasting station, spent his earnings in taking voice training and courses in radio announcing. He was given a few chances on small programs but was too colorless to attract attention. Eventually he decided to forsake broadcasting, but he still wanted to do something in radio, so he learned to play a trombone moderately well and got a job with a small band that played once in a while on some program or other. He became the band's business manager, secured a few bookings, and struggled along for about six months before admitting failure. When he was again out of work he took a job as scene shifter in a theater. He was delighted with the stir and excitement behind the scenes. Within a week he was enrolled in an extension course in dramatics. His enthusiasm once more ran high as he began to train himself to be an actor. He is still at it and is extremely annoyed over the likelihood of being drafted within a few weeks. His teachers agree that he is a pleasant, capable young man with an agreeable speaking voice, but no particular talent for the stage.

Mr. J has never outgrown his adolescence. Occupations that seem to him glamorous continue to arouse his enthusiasm. At twenty-four he has not yet shown an interest in any work for which he has adequate ability. He has never faced the fact that he is an ordinary young man who has an appreciation of the aesthetic but no specific talent. He is content with dead-end jobs that leave him free time for pursuing his most recent enthusiasm. He lives in a tiny room, eats little, works at tasks below his mental level, and eschews all vices. Thus far his life has been utterly harmless and utterly impractical. It is to be hoped that army discipline may succeed where civilian laissez-faire has failed. Mr. J may emerge from the army a man instead of an overage boy.

This young man is still proceeding upon the childish principle that enthusiasm compensates for defects. In fact, he does not yet assess himself objectively enough to know that he has defects.

Making a compromise with life is essential to growing up, and the capacity to do so does not seem to have much relation to innate ability. It may even be that the more complex a person is, the less easily he can work out a compromise. The typical adolescent with a dozen interests and a dozen urges in different directions, who tries to pursue every interest and satisfy every urge all at once, is the epitome of one who does not compromise at all. He plays tennis, baseball, golf, and ice hockey; he swims, fences, and skates; he is in the senior play, on two dance committees, and is chairman of a program committee; he tinkers with the car, the radio, the electricity, and the plumbing; he plays bridge, gin rummy, checkers, and poker; he belongs to four clubs; he has a girl whom he takes to dances and movies; he collects stamps, rocks, and candid-camera shots; he is taking lessons on the piano, the accordion, and in tap dancing; he has a job as delivery boy on Saturdays; he sings in the church choir, attends Sunday school, and goes to the Christian Endeavor. In short, he makes no compromise whatever. As he grows older, he will either work out a solution or have one forced on him.

INTELLECTUAL MATURITY

One of my acquaintances is a bright young man of twenty-six who has in popular parlance not yet found himself. He has some half-dozen burning interests that are consuming his energy and physical strength. At present he weighs barely 100 pounds although he is of average height. He has no routine, but pursues one or another activity as the spirit moves him. His breakfast hour varies from 6 a.m. to 6 p.m., and he misses half his meals because he is busy doing something else. Some nights he sleeps two hours and some, twelve. Nothing in his life has either stability or security. He will not, however, give up any of his interests. He studies Arabic, composes music, goes on archeological field trips, is an ordained minister and substitutes in nearby parishes, works three days a week as a jeweler, and gives fencing lessons. He is sacrificing his health rather than grow up and limit himself to a single vocation and one or two avocations. Thus far he continues to take a youthful delight in being able to do everything, but the day is not far distant when a nervous collapse will force a decision upon him.

A compromise with life does not involve a loss of personality or the settling down to a drab existence. It consists of fitting the pattern to the cloth as well as you can with what you have, instead of trying to stretch the cloth to cover a more elaborate pattern; it may stretch a little, but pulled too far it will only tear. The two men described below had probably inferior ability, but their compromise with life was perhaps better than yours or mine.

I remember some years ago riding out to Boulder Dam with a young man who worked there. On the way we got into a conversation about the project, and I asked him what he did. He replied simply but proudly, "I'm a carpenter." Further inquiry revealed that he spent his days making the wooden frames into which concrete is poured.

He enlarged upon the accuracy demanded by this task and the need to be an expert before attempting it. Recently he had found a new and quicker way of managing some detail of construction and had since been promoted. Under encouragement he talked in glowing terms of the intricacies and difficulties one had to overcome. To be sure his English showed lapses from grammatical perfection, but his enthusiasm was spontaneous and real. Upon discovering that I was a schoolteacher, he said he had originally intended to be one, but that a semester in normal school had convinced him he was not well fitted for such work. He expressed no disappointment, nor did he seem to harbor any consciousness of failure. He obviously mentioned the matter merely to keep up his end of the conversation. His vocational compromise, at least, seemed excellent. He liked carpentry, he did his work well, and he had a fundamental interest in it.

Mr. H is almost an institution in the small city where he lives. As nearly as his occupation could be classified, he would be called a handyman. He mows lawns, weeds gardens, and washes windows in the summer, in the winter he fixes electrical gadgets that refuse to work, tends the furnaces, and shovels snow. In addition to these routine activities, he builds almost anything from a bird-house to a bookcase, or from a flagstone walk to a brick wall. His work is not especially ingenious, but it is well done. He tends to minutiae with loving care, measures from all angles, planes and sandpapers each board before using it, and spends hours in getting each detail exactly right. The remarkable thing about Mr. H is not however his workmanship but his pride in each thing he finishes. If it is portable, he carries it around the neighborhood and shows it to the families for whom he works. If it is not portable, he persuades his numerous employers to come and see what he has done. He does not want to be praised or complimented. What he wants is to have others enjoy the perfection of the thing he has built. He once escorted me six

INTELLECTUAL MATURITY

blocks to show me three brick steps he had built to replace some wooden ones that had broken. The point he wanted admired was the absolute evenness and straightness of the steps from any angle whatever. The fact that he had made them was not as important to him as the accuracy of the work. Throughout one section of the city there are lawns Mr. H has planted and tended, garages he has built or rebuilt, roofs he has shingled, shrubs he has transplanted, fences he has put up, and houses he has painted. His progress through the neighborhood is rather deliberate, because he stops in front of every fourth or fifth house to enjoy the fruits of his labors. Mr. H is neither conceited nor boastful; he has only an honest pride in simple work that is carefully done. In his humble way he has left more of an imprint upon the life of the community than many a man of more spectacular talents. Moreover, he is one of the happiest people I know.

The probable mental inferiority of these two men has not prevented them from growing up. They have made their compromise with life and they are happy.

An adult does not close his mind permanently, except perhaps on a few fundamental moral issues, nor does he even close it temporarily until he is sure the available evidence is all in. He is willing to investigate in order to find an answer, or to withhold his conclusion while others investigate. Recently I happened to mention to an acquaintance that in a certain college the professors were to be rated each semester by their students. "Well, that's a waste of time," my acquaintance replied, "The students' ratings will exactly correspond to the marks they get." His was a mind that was neatly made up on the basis of no evidence whatever. When I told him that at least a dozen reliable investigators had proved beyond the shadow of a doubt that there was no relation between marks and ratings, he took refuge from the necessity of adjusting to evidence by a pointblank refusal to believe it. The people who conclude that all blondes are intellectual lightweights because they once happened to know a blonde who was not too well endowed mentally, or that all dogs are vicious because one once bit the grocery boy, are showing their mental immaturity by closing their minds after one observation. Drawing a conclusion without evidence, on too little evidence, or on the basis of a single dramatic incident, are all childish habits, indulged in largely because children cannot wait for more data to appear. An adult not only can keep his mind open; he does. Not so, however, one scholar of distinction:

About a year ago a friend of mine received a most unusual letter from a Dr. S, to whose work he had had occasion to refer in print. The reference had been appreciative and polite, but discriminatory rather than laudatory. Dr. S was not in the least grateful for the numerous nice things my friend had said about him and his work; rather he was furious, because he had not been regarded as a messiah with a vital scientific message. His letter was full of defensive statements about "my point of view," "my contributions," "my school of thought," "my philosophy," "my research," and so on, but his outstanding objection was voiced in the following words: "You have had the audacity to trace what you call my development. Let me tell you that in 1906 I made up my mind on all these issues and I have never changed it since, nor shall I change it." The whole tone of the letter was one of childish rage at not being considered the center of the universe, but the

INTELLECTUAL MATURITY

above statement shows an equal immaturity in purely intellectual attitudes.

Finally a true adult knows that the universe is indifferent to his fate, and he can face this fact without hysterics. This attitude, if adopted at all, comes with maturity. The college student who explained to me on December 7, 1941, "There *can't* be a war! My boy friend and I are going to be married next June," was hardly out of her intellectual babyhood. The agony which grips many people as they watch soldiers go up the gangplank of a boat that will carry them into danger comes largely from the inability to admit the indifference of life to any one person's destiny. Until the great disillusionment takes place and one becomes reconciled to being insignificant, one remains a child, no matter how vast his store of intellectual treasures may become.

In my opinion then, six different intellectual traits distinguish the adult from the child or the adolescent. A mature person can come to a decision without having it bolstered up by friends, tradition, relatives, or authority; he can see that the tail goes with the hide, and he regularly applies this knowledge to his own activities; he can observe himself without being overwhelmed by prejudice; he prefers making a compromise to butting his head against a wall; he does not make up his mind in advance of the evidence; and he knows full well that he is not important.

CHAPTER 4

Emotional Maturity

THE PSYCHOLOGIST will tell the earnest seeker that the outstanding emotional difference between an adult and a child is the ability of the former to bear tension. Put in simpler English, an adult can carry a load of emotional strain without blowing up under it and can inhibit his normal reactions for a long time. When a small child is angry he strikes out at once and discharges his anger, thus relieving his emotional tension. An adult can be angry for quite a while without showing it much, and he can postpone his outburst to a convenient time when it will not interfere too much with business. It is a psychological maxim that an emotion will find an expression, sooner or later, direct or indirect; but a grown person can choose the time and nature of the expression. Instead of bawling out the office force, a business man who has been cheated out of an important contract can bottle his anger temporarily, treat his innocent employees civilly, and then work off his anger playing a fast game of handball. Quite different is the behavior of one acquaintance, an unusually competent trial lawyer, who gets into towering rages, fires his clerks, and calls up every-

EMOTIONAL MATURITY

one he can think of on the telephone—sometimes to rave at them, sometimes to get their sympathy. There have been occasions when he was unable to indulge in his simple telephonic pleasures because he was so abusive to the switchboard girls that their supervisor ordered them to ignore his calls. Such manifestations are not only bad-mannered; they are childish and on a par with the behavior of a small boy who throws himself on the floor and screams. Temper tantrums are normal for a four-year-old child, but by the time the child is an adolescent they are already definitely abnormal. In the case of an adult a temper tantrum is evidence of only an infantile capacity to bear the stress and strain of life.

I have one acquaintance who is an almost perfect example of emotional retardation. In her childhood days she used to scream whenever she did not get her own way. Many mothers in the neighborhood did not like their daughters to play with little Marjorie because she was so uninhibited that she sometimes struck and injured other children. Even in her high school days, Marjorie still had some outbursts in class and worse ones at home. I can remember how, on the evening of our senior prom, she stood in her front hall stamping her feet and yelling curses, until her mother finally handed over an expensive fur wrap that Marjorie had decided she was going to wear. Since Marjorie has been married she has gotten worse. To be sure her husband has a great fondness for teasing and for practical jokes. He likes to see her get angry and deliberately goads her. Within the past two years—she is now over forty—I have seen her throw herself on the floor and scream with rage. Normally, however, her outbursts take the form of writing inexcusable letters, which she generally soon regrets sending. This woman has a degree of control about equal to that of a first-grade child. She learned early to get her own way by making scenes and failed therefore to acquire normal self-control. Many of her present outbursts are for the purpose of getting her own way, although some come from other causes.

A true adult differs from either a child or an adolescent in his susceptibility to certain stimuli and his resistance to others. Consider, for instance, the most typical sources of worry, fear, or anxiety at different age levels.

Infancy: being dropped, loud noises.
Early Childhood: strange animals, thunder, the dark.
Later Childhood: being kidnapped, robbed, or injured, ghosts, floods, storms, fire.
Early Adolescence: being unpopular, being "different," being dressed inappropriately, being dominated in the home.
Later Adolescence: clothes, love affairs, money, getting a job.
Early Adulthood: marriage, economic independence.
Later Adulthood: economic insecurity, sickness or want in the family, provision for old age.

Each age has its own anxieties, its own interests, its own sources of pleasure, and its own problems that are normal to it, but the emotional stimuli of one period should not continue to be important at later age levels. I know one forty-year-old woman who will wait outside her house under a street lamp until some member of her family comes home, rather than enter a dark house alone. Usually when she goes out in the afternoon and does not expect to return until late, she turns on half a dozen electric lights in broad daylight before leaving. To say that she has a phobia of the dark explains nothing; nor is it too convincing to say that she once had a frightening experience in the dark, because most people have had at least one such experience without developing a phobia. It is a simpler explanation that her parents never educated her out of a fear that was once normal, and she has never educated herself out of it since reaching years of supposed discretion. People show their emotional age quite as much in the stimuli to which they react as they do in the speed and nature of their reactions. The incident described below, which occurred at a neighbor's house during my childhood, illustrates how different stimuli affect people at different ages.

The sixteen-year-old boy in a neighbor's family had asked his history teacher, a man of about fifty, to the house for dinner. As the hour for the teacher's arrival drew near, the boy called his ten-year-old sister, saw that she put on a clean dress, lectured her on being a lady, parked her in the swing on the front porch, and ordered her to sit there and stay clean, if she could. The lad was in his own room putting the finishing touches to his own toilet, when his small sister spied the teacher approaching the house. Being on her good behavior, the child went to meet him and, because she wanted to be especially nice, asked him to come in through the back door and kitchen, on the principle that this method of entrance was more informal and friendly. Both the mother of the family and the teacher were a bit surprised to come face to face in a small back hall generously cluttered with overcoats and rubbers, but neither was especially disturbed. The adolescent boy, however, was furious. For him the evening was ruined because the mores had been so outraged. He scolded his sister until she dissolved in tears, and his mother intervened. The two children were finally separated, but the boy remained angry and sullen, especially after his mother refused to punish her small daughter since the latter had acted with the best intentions. The little girl, who adored her big brother, was too brokenhearted to eat. She sat at the table alternately sniveling and bursting out with angry words of self-defense. The adults tried to behave as if nothing had happened but without conspicuous success. As the dinner party continued, the parents became greatly annoyed at their children's behavior, and the teacher grew embarrassed at their annoyance. By the end of the meal the teacher was angry at the parents for making him uncomfortable, the parents were angry at the children, and the children were angry at each other.

Adolescents are notably unstable in their emotional reactions and they are given to moods. This behavior is the result both of the glandular imbalance that comes during the period of physical maturing and of the pressure caused by a too-complex social life. In most cases, however, an adolescent enjoys being emotionally unstable and deliberately seeks stimuli of an exciting nature. Adolescents like nothing better than to have their emotional equilibrium upset. Hence the popularity of the movies. As one grows older, the movies cease to thrill and become merely diverting, a sign that one has reached emotional adulthood. Indeed the whole search for a thrill of whatever nature is a concomitant of the adolescent years. An adult wants stability and had rather be spared the emotional wallowing of the young.

It is obvious that a proportion of the adult population is retarded in its emotional growth. Consider, for instance, the forty-year-old woman who loaned me a copy of *The Rosary* bound in tooled leather and told me I must be supercareful of it because it was her greatest treasure. At sixteen a passion for sentimental novels is perfectly normal, but not at forty. Another acquaintance of mine has kept unchanged for over thirty years the room in which her small son lived and died. His toys are dusted every week and then put back on the floor where he dropped them, his clothes still hang in the closet, and a book he was reading an hour before his death lies open on the table. A few more typical examples of emotional immaturity appear below.

Miss R is an extremely intelligent woman but also a decidedly homely one. In her girlhood, before she learned that severely tailored clothes gave her a look of distinction, she used to dress in the ruffles and furbelows that embellished the youthful freshness of other girls, but made her look like the wrath of God. It is not surprising that she won scholarships instead of beaux. Her appearance failed to attract most men, and her brilliance scared to death the few whom she managed to meet. She grew up into a superior type of woman executive and is, in most ways, thoroughly adult. She has, however, one outstanding adolescent trait that keeps her friends in a continual state of anxiety, for fear it will lead her into real trouble some day.

About once in two years Miss R falls more or less seriously in love. Sometimes she develops only a passing fancy, but one attack in every four or five is serious. She is quite catholic in her tastes and has centered her affections upon young girls, young men, both men and women of her own age, and upon distinctly elderly men. In fact, she can fall in love with almost anyone. Her affairs so far as is known have not reached the stage of sexual completion, which could prove to be a solution, but they are certainly disrupting to everyone who comes in contact with her during one of her consuming devotions. The episodes have a definite pattern. First Miss R begins to talk continually about someone she has just met, bringing the person's name into the conversation in every other sentence, quoting what he or she has said, and often misquoting by putting her own really witty speech in her idol's mouth. After a week or so of these preliminaries, she begins to invite the object of her interest to her house for dinner, to her office for conferences, and to her club for tea. At first the person is usually enchanted, for Miss R can be fascinating, interesting, and exciting. Also she has a position that makes friendship with her worth while from a practical point of view. Throughout the early stages of her affairs she shows a severe case of hero-worship and ascribes to her new friend the virtues of any two saints. Soon, however, she becomes so importunate in her demands upon her idol's time, interest, and attention that she smothers any affection she might earlier have kindled. As the other person withdraws from the situation, sometimes gracefully and sometimes with an elephantine tread, she at first pursues more actively and then gradually realizes that the end has once more arrived. She subsides into a mood of melancholy that lasts for a few days and then emerges as her normal, cheerful, intelligent, industrious, and charming self.

These episodes show the same pattern as the combined puppy-love and hero-worship of a thirteen- or fourteen-year-old girl. Miss R's emotional immaturity has not only led her into ridiculous situations, but has nearly cost her her job during the three or four periods when she was not merely attracted to someone but in love up to her neck. In this condition she has neglected her work, has gotten into quarrels with anyone who criticized her, and has been more or less a storm center.

Of late years—she is now well over sixty—the fires of

love have finally begun to burn a little less brightly and Miss R has, to the infinite relief of her real friends, transferred such embers as still glow from humans to cats. It is a little tiresome to listen to her chatter about pussy, but even that is preferable to a continual dread of her involvement in a thoroughgoing scandal.

Mr. J was once the outstanding student of his small college, which he entered at the age of fifteen, a boy in short pants. He took to languages like a duck to water and became a fine linguist, but he has never developed into the college professor and scholar everyone predicted. Instead he is a court interpreter.

As early as his high school days Mr. J began to restrict his social contacts to those who were his chronological age, instead of making friends among his classmates. In his first two college years his chum was another sixteen-year-old in the ninth grade. Mr. J definitely liked grown women, but he was afraid of well-bred, nice, young girls. As the years passed, the disparity between his intellectual development and his emotional interests became greater and greater, and he was less and less able to get along with his peers of either sex. He taught at his alma mater as assistant for several years after graduation, but when it became evident that he was not going to mature socially he was dropped. His present work is far below his mental capacity, but it makes no social demands that he cannot meet.

Emotionally Mr. J is still in his adolescent years. He spends much time at a boys' club where he is supposed to be a sort of counselor, but actually pals around with the boys as an agemate. He likes nothing better than to get a group of youngsters together, talk and sing with them, and be the life of the party. He has great interest in his Sunday-school class of adolescent boys and often takes juvenile court cases home with him for a few months and is quite successful in reforming them. Socially Mr. J is well adjusted to adolescence, but among adults he is most uncomfortable. He blushes, stammers, overstays his welcome, does not know how to leave gracefully, and has only the most rudimentary ideas about adult conversation. Either he lectures others, carefully talking down to them, or else he sits in a hurt and aloof silence. His interests are centered upon the things that interest adolescent boys.

One might at first assume that Mr. J was homosexual, but he is not mature enough emotionally to have reached even that stage. His attachments were for many years to women old enough to be his mother and he continues to like them, but of late he has begun to associate with girls in their late adolescent years. Those to whom he devotes his attention quite clearly already know their way around. They may be chronologically twenty years younger than he, but emotionally they are considerably more mature and experienced. Mr. J once married a woman twice his age, but the marriage did not last. His wife was a garish, painted, bedizened creature who would not have fooled a normal boy of sixteen.

Until recently Mr. J has been in a childish state of dependence for emotional satisfaction upon an older woman, presumably a mother-substitute in his emotional life. From her he wanted not only affection but protection and guidance. Now that he is forty years old and those women old enough to be mother-substitutes to him are elderly, he has been seeking the same guidance from girls whose social age is approximately his own but who are experienced enough in matters of love to dominate him. They are in effect almost as much mother-substitutes as the older women he cared for earlier, but their social maturity does not overwhelm him with the stagefright he experiences in social relationships with adults. The great discrepancy between this man's emotional and intellectual development, precipitated probably by his inexcusably rapid advancement in school, has cost society a first-rate scholar and has produced an immature, maladjusted, unhappy human being.

EMOTIONAL MATURITY

Miss Finney was an odd little person who lived near me in my youth, flitted like a shadow about the neighborhood, and was usually engaged in a mild way in what could be called good works. She was completely unobtrusive. In fact I developed a childhood anxiety that some day harmless Miss Finney would get locked in a closet and no one would miss her for a week. Few people so much as saw Miss Finney, but some question or bewilderment in the back of her eyes used to make me wonder what had happened to produce an elderly nonentity from what should have been a rather pretty, delicate, youngish woman. One rainy day I found part of the answer. Miss Finney's niece and I were amusing ourselves in the attic looking at some old picture albums. In one of them I found a series of pictures showing a young, happy, fragile-looking Miss Finney. In those pictures there was serenity and trust in her eyes, not bewilderment. The last picture of the series showed Miss Finney and a young man in an officer's uniform. I asked the niece who he was, and she replied that he had been Auntie's beau who was killed in the Spanish-American war. Some years later, as I was taking flowers to our family lot in the local cemetery, I happened to see Miss Finney standing before a tombstone. She did not notice me, and I went on about my errand, but on the way back to the graveyard gates I found that Miss Finney had fainted. By the time I reached her she was already reviving, but she was not yet her usual controlled self. With a shaking finger she pointed to the tombstone and cried, "Do you see that date? That's the day I died. Oh yes, he died too, but I might as well have been put here with him." Presently she composed herself and I helped her get home and to bed.

The brother with whom she lived thanked me later and told me that he had forgotten the date or he would have been with her, "Because," said he, "this is the anniversary of her fiancé's death. She always spends the day at his grave and has to be helped home. I thought she'd outgrow her sorrow, but she never has."

From these scattered references and incidents, I can piece together the essential elements of an all-too-common story. A delicate and retiring girl lost her soldier-fiancé in a war. One would naturally expect a period of mourning, but in the course of time a recovery should have followed. Miss Finney simply never took up her life again. She assumed the adolescent attitude that her tragedy was a unique experience, from which no recovery was possible.

Many young women have had a similar bereavement. Although they may have carried memories and regrets for some years they have resumed their lives, become mature people, married, and been useful members of their community. Eventually, their youthful heartbreak has faded until they have almost forgotten it—and even when recalled the experience has lost most of its power to hurt. Only a perennial adolescent can retain for twenty years a sentimental interest in a dead man. Miss Finney looked older than she was, but within she was still just sweet sixteen. She had sacrificed herself rather than face life and grow up into an adult.

Mrs. W is now over fifty. Her husband is dead and she never had any children. In her youth she went to a small school where she did only mediocre classwork but had a glorious time. Mrs. W was not a popular student in her own right, but she basked in the reflected glory of a sister who had been a great leader in school affairs. After graduation Mrs. W had married one of her sister's cast-off beaux. He was a wealthy man upon whom she prevailed to make large donations to her former school. Eventually he became a trustee. Mrs. W never missed a reunion or other gathering of the alumnae. In addition she often returned to school for a visit, frequently remaining for several weeks. She knew almost every girl in every class, entertained students in her rooms, and was entranced by their chatter. After her husband's death she rented a house near the school grounds and has lived there ever since. The girls stream in and out of her house, accepting her hospitality but making slurring comments about her among themselves. Since she will probably leave her considerable fortune to the school the authorities do not care to interfere with her harmless but rather silly contacts with the students. When she is with them nothing but her gray hair and matronly figure distinguishes her from them. Her conversation consists chiefly of anecdotes about students past or present. She giggles at the girls' witticisms, admires their talents, and follows their careers. To her agemates she is an utter bore. She never tires of telling how she was once caught eating bread and jam in the chemistry laboratory or how her sister held three important student offices at once.

Mrs. W is by no means a fool in spite of her obsessions about student life. She handles her own investments shrewdly, gives excellent addresses before clubs when the school wants to raise money, dresses well, and manages her house with taste and skill. It is in her social development that she is retarded. In the midst of adolescent chaff and humor she is at home; in an adult conversation she is confused and uncomfortable. She has no friends of her own age, but many adolescent girls find in her a person who is comfortably older in worldly wisdom and comfortably adolescent in interests and enthusiasm.

An adult level of emotional development seems to me to contain three main elements: an ability to bear tension, an indifference toward the kinds of stimuli that move the child or the adolescent, and an outgrowing of adolescent moodiness and sentimentality. These characteristics may seem general and vague but with practice one can learn to recognize them. To a psychologist or psychiatrist they are as obvious as a goitre is to a doctor. On the whole, emotional retardation is more frequent than any other type, perhaps because there is little direct education of the emotions in the average school. Such training as children get is incidental. Presumably a more direct approach would produce in the next generation a greater proportion of adults with mature emotional responses, since such reactions are highly modifiable.

CHAPTER 5

Social Maturity

THE PERSON who is socially adult is not hard to recognize. He has achieved independence from his home, he has found security in friendships among his agemates, he has settled upon a stable sexual pattern, he has made an adjustment to accepted customs and conventions, and he has found work that interests him. In general, mankind has greater success in developing adult social reactions than in other phases of growing up.

Freedom from home domination does not mean a deliberate or violent breach with parents. It means merely that one has become as independent of them as of other people, however affectionately one may regard them. Circumstances usually force young men and women out of their homes by the time they reach adulthood. College, marriage, or a job in another place effect a break with the home and necessitate a beginning of social as well as financial independence. There are, however, two common types of immature reaction to the problem of achieving independence from parental supervision: the submissive person who is as dependent upon his parents as the average child, and the person who is in a state of flaming revolt against his home. The latter may refuse to go near the place or even to let his parents know where he is; he may or may not send them money out of a sense of duty, but he has little kindly feeling toward them. The one type is just as immature as the other. Neither can treat parents as friends. In one case, the parents are still the beloved tyrants of childhood and in the other they are the heartless ogres of the adolescent in revolt. The true adult is on terms of independent friendship with his parents, and he neither leans on them nor fights them. Such unemancipated individuals as those I am about to describe are to be found among everybody's acquaintances.

Marshall was a sophisticated smart-aleck. In general, his behavior was aggressive, quarrelsome, and impolite toward the foreman of his shop, although he seemed to get along well enough with most of his agemates. He began work at a time when the shop was undergoing a period of reorganization and upheaval. The situation naturally produced tension and frayed nerves. The younger workers did not understand what the excitement was all about, but some of the bolder spirits among them thought the time a good one for getting their own way about this or that situation that had previously irked them. Consequently, there were several minor strikes, of varying proportions and for varying causes. Marshall had no personal reason for interesting himself in the situation. On his own testimony, he liked his work. Yet he was in the forefront of every strike. He got up and made speeches, urging other workers into even more open revolt, he injected personalities into his comments, he offered to debate the issues publicly with any member of the firm who cared to oppose him. Labor was scarce and Marshall was an excellent worker, so the first few outbursts on his part were overlooked. Presently, however, the distracted foreman and firm officials came to feel that Marshall was the center of the disaffection.

Marshall's foreman was a firm believer in the theory that waywardness is a result of maladjustment; instead of discharging Marshall he sent him to a personnel officer for examination. For some time the interview did not progress at all, because Marshall's attitudes were so covered by a veneer of sophistication and bad manners that his underlying adjustments could not be seen. Since questions about this situation at the shop merely aroused Marshall's aggressiveness, the personnel officer tried some general questions about the young man's home and family. On this topic Marshall was both expansive and abusive. He quite clearly adored his mother, although he tried to conceal it, and was fond of his two sisters, but he hated his father with a deadly hatred. The basis for this attitude was not far to seek. His father was a chronic drunkard who was quarrelsome at all times and at intervals cruelly abusive to the women of the family. Marshall had spent his boyhood in repeated and useless attempts to defend his mother and sisters from his father. He had seen them knocked down and maltreated. For some years the father had not lived regularly with the family, but he had returned occasionally, and there had been fights with Marshall, who was by now big enough to give his father quite an argument. One of the things that had infuriated Marshall ever since he could remember was that this man whom he detested should have the authority in the eyes of the world to order him around. Until he could defend himself by actual physical combat, he had to do as he was told. With this history, it was not hard to see why Marshall flared up at the first hint of oppression. No matter how pleasant foremen or other officials might be, they represented authority. The boy was on the side of the strikers, not because he had complaints but because he was fundamentally against control from above. Marshall comes from a kind of home in which the chronic "anti's" are developed. He did not care what the issues involved in an argument were—he was merely against the side that represented authority.

The foreman was greatly interested in the personnel officer's report. Before he had time to take action on it, he received news that the boy's father had been killed in a drunken brawl. The immediate cause of Marshall's attitude was therefore removed, but the foreman realized that the young man must be re-educated or the attitude would continue. He therefore persuaded Marshall to come and live with him for a while, renting an attic room that happened to be vacant. He reasoned quite correctly that what Marshall needed was to live with a decent, older man, in a home in which girls and women were properly treated. Marshall knew well no adult man except his father and without realizing it he had built up an erroneous picture of male maturity. He lived with the foreman for nearly a year and then returned to his own family. Although Marshall is still a little too quick to resent the touch of authority, his basic attitude has changed a good deal. And his manners have undergone practically a revolution; he is pleasant, polite, and inoffensive, insofar as everyday contacts are concerned. Marshall has a grasp of the situation himself, and is trying to offset the resentment to authority generated by his father's behavior.

Mr. B is a young man of thirty-two, the only child of a widowed mother. When Mr. B graduated from high school he entered his father's business as a bookkeeper. A year later his father died. Mr. B had always been abnormally attached to his mother upon whom he depended for all kinds of help. His mother kept his clothes in order, bought everything for him, was his constant companion, read aloud to him in the evening, cooked his favorite foods, adjusted her time to suit his, helped him with extra work when necessary, read and abstracted professional books, kept his bank account, wrote his checks, made his appointments, sent him at intervals to the dentist, chose the few acquaintances she allowed him, and was the center of his life. The young man had never had a girl, nor had he felt the need of feminine friends except his mother. Two years ago the mother died. The emotional shock was severe, but the practical results were even worse. Mr. B could not tie his own necktie, shine his shoes, or even find his belongings. He did not know how much razor blades, soap, or tooth paste cost because he had never bought them. He had no idea what his current expenses were. He had no friends to whom he could turn. Without his mother's constant supervision he got behind in his office work and soon lost his job. His clothes became shabby, but he did not know where to get more or how much he should pay for them. The childishness of this man's behavior is too obvious to require comment.

Foster is a very bright young man of twenty-five and a Grade A pest. In the office where he is a clerk he is always talkative, often deliberately mischievous, and frequently unable to guide his own activities. A few minutes after the other clerks have opened their desks and started to work, Foster is running around the office asking where he is supposed to begin. Presently he encounters a minor difficulty and asks a friend what to do. If told to read his instructions he is again in trouble because he either cannot find the directions or will not read them carefully enough to understand them. He wants someone to tell him the meaning. At the end of an hour he has perhaps done fifteen minutes' work, has interrupted other people several times, has been to the head clerk with two or three questions, has been to the washroom once or twice, and has chattered with friends en route during each pilgrimage. In contrast to his inefficient work at the office, the material he takes home to work on in the evenings is always well done. Every evening his parents go over his papers with him and not only help him but give him the intimate supervision he has to have if he is to concentrate on what he is doing. Recently the head clerk has realized Foster's dependence upon older people and has solved the problem of his inattention by giving him a desk adjoining her own and by allowing him to interrupt her twenty times a day. Now that he receives the special indulgence he craves, he does good work and is well behaved. This treatment will not, however, solve Foster's problems, because the head clerk is in self-defense strengthening those very reactions that are already too strong. The situation is a difficult one. If the boss insists upon trying to push Foster into greater independence, she will neglect other clerks and decrease the efficiency of her office force; if she pampers him, she not only prevents him from growing up but uses time and energy that should be given to others in the group. Talking to Foster and pointing out to him the childishness of his reactions might do a little good, but each step toward independence during office hours is more likely than not to be offset by the smothering attention given him at home. It is probable that Foster will go on through life demanding from his employers, friends, and wife the same comforting guidance that a small child has every right to expect from his parents.

One of my acquaintances, Mary M., has developed an almost perfect adjustment to life on a childish level, even though she is now a woman of forty. According to her own statement, she solves problems as they arise by deciding what her mother would have done and then doing it. In her work as head bookkeeper in a large concern she is competent and successful. The one unfavorable comment her subordinates have to make about her is that she tends to mother them too much and to interfere in their lives, although they admit that her interference springs from the kindliest of motives. Mary M.'s mother was not merely somewhat dominating but brilliant, warm, exciting, and attractive. She could not help being the center of every group or being the ruling member of her family. Less capable people simply gravitated toward her, put their problems in her hands, and let her solve them. Mary M.

probably had only average ability to start with and she early developed a tendency to intense hero-worship—incidentally, thus eliminating the strain that might have arisen between her and those who were brighter. Her deepest admiration was centered upon the most scintillating person in her immediate environment, her mother, whose vivid personality still survives, although she has been dead for many years. In small things as in large Mary M. is still her mother's little girl. For instance she will not use cheese that is already grated because her mother said it always got dry, as it probably did since her mother lived in pre-cellophane days. She makes an ordinary gelatine pudding by a complicated process that was necessary before the days of easily dissolved gelatine. She never roasts chickens because her mother always casseroled them, and she refuses to use powdered soap, which her mother always referred to contemptuously as "lazy woman's soap." One is sometimes surprised by Mary M's habit of making pungent and trenchant remarks that are quite out of keeping with her mild and inoffensive personality unless one knows that she is merely quoting her mother verbatim. Mother tossed off such comments and promptly forgot them, but her daughter carefully wrote them down and memorized them.

This woman thinks she has few problems of adjustment because she settles each question as it arises through application of the childish criteria by which she lives. Thus far she has made good her voluntary escape from maturity into the remembered shelter of her mother's arms. Although Mary M. senses no problems, to the psychiatrist her entire design for living presents a problem of staggering proportions.

The typical adult does not have a great number of friends because he does not have much time to devote either to the consolidation of old acquaintanceships or the development of new ones. He does, however, have a circle of intimates among whom he holds a secure and established place. The adult male plays poker or golf with his pals, accompanies them to the ball game, and participates with them in an occasional mild binge. The adult woman goes shopping or to the movies with her friends, plays bridge with them, invites them to her house for tea, exchanges anecdotes about her children and home life generally, and holds long, gossipy, unimportant conversations with them over the telephone—to the great disgust of anyone who shares the line. Married couples exchange dinner dates and often belong to the same club with other congenial couples of about the same age. The adult who is isolated from this normal, pleasant, and unexciting life is definitely maladjusted and has not yet found his place in the social world about him. The recluse often clings to a childish fear of strangers and therefore does not venture upon those initial contacts that eventually ripen into friendships.

A true adult has found some stable sexual pattern that satisfies him. The overwhelming majority of people find marriage and monogamy the solution of this problem, and most marriages are monogamous because the arrangement gives the stability that adults want. Other people develop patterns that may be less permanent but which give security for a while—heterosexual attachments without marriage, homosexual relationships, or masturbation. While these are not entirely mature manifestations of sexual interest, they are better than promiscuity, the most infantile form of expression. Promiscuous

SOCIAL MATURITY

adults are thirteen- or fourteen-year-olds who are so insecure in their emotional and social worlds that they grasp at every fleeting thrill, substituting excitement for safety and thus preventing themselves from ever growing up. People who do not marry, do not have affairs, and rarely masturbate usually achieve an adjustment called sublimation; that is, the sexual drives become harnessed to other interests and work themselves out without any overt sexual behavior whatever. The stock example of this adjustment is the spinster schoolteacher who loses herself in the problems and lives of her pupils. Her life seems to her exciting and full of interest, and she has no consciousness of deprivation.

People may fail to reach a stable sexual adjustment for any of a number of reasons or they may reach it only after numerous false starts. The matter of inadequate or abnormal adjustment has furnished the central themes of so many problem plays and novels that the average reader is already fairly familiar with the common solutions of such problems. However it seems desirable to present some brief histories from real life; if they seem dull, perhaps the reader will remember that life is not art. I could probably make these nonfictional characters more interesting, if I were allowed to weave a few strands of fantasy about them. The reader should notice the underlying reasons for a failure to grow up into normal heterosexuality and the nature of the substitutes found.

Elaine, a woman of thirty-two, was the youngest of three sisters. Her father died soon after her birth. The mother and the three girls then went to live with an aunt who was a missionary in China. At the mission there were other white women but no men. The girls were not allowed to play with native children. When Elaine was fifteen she returned to this country to go to a boarding school in an eastern state. The rules there were strict. She saw no boys and she spent her vacations at the school with two or three equally isolated girls. After two years she entered a woman's college. At both boarding school and college she was conspicuous for her crushes. At one time she fell in love with her history teacher, spent several entire nights sitting outside the woman's door, dogged her footsteps in the daytime, wrote her letters, talked of her continually, until the other girls became too bored to listen. This affair lasted about six weeks during which she was so emotionally upset that she lost over fifteen pounds. Later she developed an equally intensive crush on a senior girl but in this case the feeling was mutual. The two girls were not allowed to room together although they managed to spend almost the entire twenty-four hours of almost every day with each other. After graduating Elaine returned to her alma mater as an assistant. Several other crushes occurred. Finally, at the age of twenty-nine, she decided to get a Ph.D. and matriculated at a large state university.

There are few women majors in physics, which was her department, so that she was for the first time in her life in classes with men. At first she treated them with utter scorn. Two or three advances toward girls and women failed dismally and she was thrown more and more with men associates. During her second graduate year a marked change took place, and she became boy-crazy in the silliest possible fashion. She chased every man in the department, had two rather scandalous affairs, stayed out nights with men, and generally made a perfect fool of herself. Her behavior closely paralleled that of a thirteen-year-old girl who has suddenly discovered that boys are nice instead of mean. But Elaine was too old for supervision by the time she reached the same stage. As the third year of her graduate work came along she began to realize she could never get a personal recommendation from the professors in her department. She developed spasms of weeping and complaining. For months she was an utter nuisance because she insisted upon telling her troubles continually. All kinds of minor hysterical symptoms developed. Then a new young man enrolled in the physics department to get an M.A. He was several years younger than Elaine, inexperienced, fresh from a small denominational college in a rural community. Elaine fastened upon him with avidity. There was a whirlwind love affair followed by their elopement. After her marriage Elaine settled down, had two children, and is still happily married. In three years' time she grew up from the homosexuality of a normal twelve-year-old girl to the normal adult type of marital adjustment.

Some years ago I met a young man of twenty-seven who had always been protected from girls, partly by an oversolicitous mother, partly by an absorbing interest in schoolwork, and partly by being accelerated so fast in school that he was thrown with people socially too old for him. At twenty-seven John had never had a girl friend. He had begun to feel himself abnormal in this respect and had made a few tentative efforts to remedy the matter by taking two or three clerks or stenographers to the movies, treating them the while with exaggerated courtesy. Evidently he did not feel confident enough to make a date with girls from his own social class. After a few months of these tentative social contacts he met and fell in love with a young woman of about his own age—a thoroughly sophisticated girl who had had a number of affairs, more or less serious. She liked John, enjoyed his somewhat erudite conversation, and found him most useful in running errands for her. Because she usually kissed him goodnight, John assumed they were engaged. In the course of time the inevitable happened. John found out about her affairs, some of which were continuing, and was both hurt and horrified. Suddenly he realized that she was not the good and beautiful maiden he had imagined, but a rather ordinary person of far from conventional morality. This sort of episode should have taken place when John was sixteen or seventeen, living at home with his family. Falling in love with a girl who is not good enough for him is part of every intelligent boy's education, but not after he becomes a man. John's affair took place too late. Instead of getting over it and charging it up to experience, he developed a hatred for all women and now has nothing more than purely business contacts with them. At the age of sixteen he might have made a similar response, but it would hardly have lasted long. At present it bids fair to become permanent. There is a time when puppy love is educative, but after that period has gone by it is only destructive.

Many of Phil's acquaintances have wondered why he did not marry. He is a most personable and pleasant man who has many women friends, but he seems never to fall in love with any of them. He shows no signs whatever of homosexual interests. Phil's mother had died when he was a boy, and he and his father had lived together until the father died, when Phil was twenty-one. Since then he has been in some college, either as a student or as a teacher. At present he is an associate professor in a state university, where he has plenty of chances to meet all kinds of girls and women. In fact, he is with women a good deal, but he does not want more than companionship from them.

The fundamental trouble is that Phil idealizes the type of woman that he might marry but at the same time he visits prostitutes whenever necessary. These two attitudes simply will not fuse. The idealistic attitude came in part from hearing his father talk in reverent terms of the dead mother, in part from reading much romantic literature—there were few examples of modern realism in the library at home—and partly from sheer ignorance of girls. When he was about thirteen he began to admire girls, especially one damsel of fifteen whom he saw in church. For nearly two years the high spot of the week was Sunday morning when he could sit in church and watch her for nearly two hours, but he never spoke to her. This sort of worship from afar is a more or less continuous performance with him, but he still does not care a great deal about meeting his idols more than casually. In the later years of adolescence he began to visit prostitutes. As a matter of convenience to himself, he visits the same one at intervals for years, and pays her for services rendered with no more emotion than he would pay a laundress for ironing a shirt. His sex life and his friendships with women are thus completely separate. Women graduate students and teachers find Phil a charming companion with whom they feel entirely safe, as they certainly are. He would never insult them by attempting the slightest physical intimacy. He has often passed through the preliminary courting stages of interest and friendship, but he does not get any further. He has learned to his sorrow that unattached women sometimes fall in love with him, so he usually restricts his friendships to women who are already firmly attached to some other man. He keeps many faculty wives harmlessly thrilled by his attentions, and he squires other men's fiancées whenever the men happen to be out of town. He loves women, but he will probably never be in love with any one woman because his sexual drives are to him so shameful and degrading that he could never center them upon the idealized woman of his dreams.

Miss R is a brilliant woman of forty-eight. She has for years been an excellent high school teacher, one of the best in a large system. Since her adolescent days she has had three different bosom friends. The first was a childhood acquaintance with whom Miss R roomed in both boarding school and college. Both taught in the same school and continued to live together. Miss R was dominant and attractive. Many boys and men fell in love with her but none awakened the slightest response. About five years after graduation Miss R's friend met a young man to whom she became engaged. Miss R appeared to have no objections but she managed subtly to keep the marriage postponed until the man lost interest. She and her friend had a terrific row and separated, the friend to remain single all her life. Miss R was despondent for a month or two, until she found another companion, a woman ten years younger than herself. Then she again became radiant and fascinating. Eventually the second friend also fell in love. This engagement was broken three or four times, but in the end the friend married and went away. Again Miss R was disconsolate for some time. During this period she herself finally yielded to her most persistent suitor and married. She and her husband are good friends; he is deeply in love with her and has apparently decided to be content with whatever she sees fit to give him. In the second year of her marriage Miss R became interested in a girl nearly twenty years her junior, who eventually came to live with Miss R and her husband. The strangely assorted trio has remained together, but the girl—now a woman—is trying to break away. Miss R is again indulging in her skillful machinations, and the husband is trying to be deaf, dumb, and blind to the strain. There has never been any suspicion of actual sexual relations between Miss R and any of her three intimate friends. The relationship is rather what one finds between two inseparable chums twelve or thirteen years old. Miss R is not so much homosexual as preadolescent. It is to be noted that with each shift in companion Miss R is forced to select a friend whose age is further and further below her own. People of her own age are by now too mature to be interested. If the present chum leaves, Miss R, who is now nearly fifty years old, will have to attract some girl thirty to thirty-five years younger than herself or else finally grow up, which is unlikely.

The really sad thing about these various adjustments is their lack of stability and permanence. Something usually happens to break up relationships that do not have public sanction. The test of an adequate, mature, sexual adjustment is the disappearance of sex as a problem or as an active or frequent element in one's thoughts. Some adjustments are better than others because they promise greater security and greater permanence, but many persons reach adult attitudes through substitutes.

Some people will probably not agree that an acceptance of customs, conventions, traditions, and manners is a sign of adulthood. There are, however, several reasons for regarding such an acceptance as an indication of maturity. The social world is held together by conventions and customs. Without them, society promptly degenerates into the social anarchy of a frontier town. Conventions admittedly inhibit one's personal liberty, but they compensate by giving order, dignity, and safety. Without making a fetish of manners and customs, one can adjust himself to them well enough to get along in society as it is constituted. The nonconformist is typified by the Greenwich Villager who has presumably freed his soul by escaping from bourgeois respectability. It was never necessary to go to New York for this purpose for, as someone once remarked, Greenwich Village is not so much a place as a state of mind. The chief trouble with the nonconformist is that he isn't very bright. He fails to see in his revolt against society the mechanism of the escapist who is running away from something he will not face. And the fundamental trouble with his bright new world is that it will not jell, because it has no traditions or conventions to hold it together. Most people pass through a period of revolt during their youth, but they outgrow it as they discover the solid comfort of convention. The typical adult therefore recognizes manners and customs for the social lubricants they are and adjusts himself to them well enough to get along in his group, even though he may keep his tongue in his cheek.

Finally, a social adult has found work that interests and satisfies him. This statement does not mean that a worker should expect every minute of every day to be full of excitement and interest, or that he will never feel the grind of dull monotony. All jobs have their tedious phases. I have talked with many students who thought that every moment of research would be thrilling, but two weeks of tabulating scores or of running rats through a maze eight times in every twenty-four hours has cured them of their misconception. And if any innocent bystander imagines that writing a book involves no periods of nauseous dullness, I can assure him to the contrary. An adult is well adjusted to his work if he is sufficiently interested in the ends he has in view to take the monotony in his stride. The notion that there exists a job which indefinitely remains all thrill is an adolescent pipedream, and the adult who is still chasing this fata morgana has failed to emerge from his adolescence.

CHAPTER 6

Moral Maturity

It is likely that I am asking for trouble when I try to discuss the criteria of moral maturity because people vary so markedly in their opinions on all matters of morality. However the field is too important to omit, so I will set forth such conclusions as I have reached, largely on the basis of the time I have spent talking to the unmoral, the immoral, the amoral, and the morally immature in sundry clinics, courts, schools, asylums, jails, and other institutions. A view of what constitutes moral maturity arrived at by this inverse approach may not agree with the criteria of those who come to their conclusions by a more philosophical and detached route.

It seems to me that an adult ought to have a code of morals. Children often behave with extreme rectitude, but their behavior is based mainly on habit and they are quite unable to tell why they act as they do. Many of one's adult reactions are habitual also, but if challenged, one should be able to justify his behavior. Thus a child is honest because he is trained to be or is afraid not to be, while the adult is honest either because he has principles that deter him in moments of temptation or because he has discovered that honesty makes life simpler and more comfortable than dishonesty. That is, he is moral because it is silly to be anything else. Perhaps it is not too much to say that childish morals are based mainly on habit, adolescent morals mainly on lofty but rather nebulous ideals, and adult morals mainly on pragmatism, the adult being good because goodness works better than badness. In actual practice adult reactions are probably a fusion of all three elements —habits, principles, and experience. In any case a mature person should have welded his training and experience into a code that he can justify if called upon to do so and of which he is at least vaguely aware as a conditioning factor in his daily behavior.

Secondly a true adult has a philosophy of life even if he is not especially vocal about it. He has, however, some answer to the age-old questions as to what human existence is for, whence it came, and whither it is bound. His solution may not satisfy him, but he has worked out something that keeps the problem from being too pressing and too upsetting, and he is still hopeful of getting an adequate solution some day. If life has no significance and if a person has no notion of what he is in the world for, there is little point in living, as many a suicide has discovered for himself. The busy commonplace woman who believes people are put into the world to help each other and that a future life depends upon the aid given one's fellowmen here below may sometimes be a nuisance, but she has a coherent point of view that organizes life so that she can bear it and puts within her grasp the means by which she can assure herself a place among the forever-elect. Consequently life has meaning for her, and she has no fears. A philosophy of life does not need to be scintillating or novel. Indeed most such philosophies are quite banal, the really fancy ones being the property of lunatics. The proof of an adequate philosophy is that it gives peace and banishes fear. Trivial, banal, or preposterous, it is worth its weight in gold.

At the risk of being considered downright reactionary and hopelessly old-fashioned I am going to suggest that true adults have one outstanding virtue, a sense of duty. Duty may be dull, but it is necessary. The irresponsible and undependable adult is still in his moral infancy. Doing something because it ought to be done is a distinctly adult reaction although some people manage to live to a ripe old age without ever showing such behavior. One of the best samples of moral immaturity I have known is described below.

Joseph Brown is a man of about thirty-five. His personality is to some extent understandable in terms of his history. His father, although a successful artist, was a dissolute individual from whom his mother obtained a divorce when Joseph was about three years old. The mother herself was an irresponsible person who boarded Joseph and his sister with their grandmother out in the country while she worked rather intermittently in the city. She visited the children only two or three times a year and never contributed regularly to their support. When Joseph was about eight the grandmother died, and he and his sister (who was five years older) continued to live alone on the farm. The mother was not willing to have the children with her in the city because they would interfere too much with her good times, and there was no other relative to whom they could be sent. Joseph's sister was not old enough to control him, and for the next few years he did practically what he pleased. At that time his mother made a second marriage and arranged for the two children to live with her. The sister did not like her stepfather; after living with the family for a few months she eloped.

Joseph continued to live with his mother and stepfather, and seemed to be making a reasonably good adjustment. Although he had attended a country school most irregularly, he quickly made up the work he had missed and entered high school at fifteen. A year later he was severely injured in football practice. For months he was in the hospital, and was subsequently in bed for about two years. During this time he was the object of lavish devotion of both his mother and stepfather. When he was finally well enough to return to school, he felt himself too old to be a high school sophomore, so he took some tutoring and entered a trade school.

There his irresponsibility first became prominent, although it had probably always existed. His earlier environment, first on the farm with his grandmother, then with his sister, and then at home in bed, had permitted irresponsibility without serious consequences. For the first time, in trade school, he was meeting normal competition and difficulties. He remained only one semester and left without taking the final examinations. He complained that the instructors were unfair, that the work was uninteresting, and that nobody liked him. He next held half a dozen odd jobs, from none of which he was actually fired because he walked out of his own accord after giving his superior a "piece of his mind." In fact, he was always proud of having "bawled out" his superiors and of leaving his jobs voluntarily.

He next got employment as salesman for a hardware company. He had always liked to travel about and talk to people, and he usually made, at first, a rather favorable impression. For several months all went well, and Joseph's family believed he had found himself at last. During this time he married a naïve and not very intelligent country girl from a tiny hamlet in his district. She regarded Joseph as a brilliant and rising young man, much too good for her. Although she was quite unsophisticated, she was completely reliable and not afraid of hard work. The marriage started off well, and the girl's dependable nature seemed to have a stabilizing effect on Joseph's personality. Gradually, however, he became dissatisfied with his work, got into arguments with the head salesman, failed to keep appointments with customers, and became a general nuisance. As usual, he sensed almost to a minute when he was going to be discharged, wrote an angry letter to the head of the concern, marched into the head salesman's office, criticized everybody, and loudly resigned his job. After this emotional flurry he again settled down for a few months as an insurance salesman. But this job also was drawing to a close when the depression threw him out of work completely.

His wife had a horror of living on charity; she therefore got a part-time job as salesgirl during rush hours in a large store and spent the rest of the time raising vegetables, which she sold to neighborhood markets. Joseph sat around the house, nursed his grievances, and made no effort to get work. At about this time he met some Italian friends who were Fascist supporters, and he became greatly interested in Italy. While his wife worked fourteen hours a day, he read every book he could find on modern Italy, talked with his enthusiastic friends, and made plans for a visit to their relatives in Italy. All of this seemed a mere daydream, but at this moment an uncle died and left him five hundred dollars. In spite of his wife's pleading, he spent this money making a visit to Italy. As he had been warned by others before he started, his friends' relatives did not like him and he did not like them. It annoyed him that they talked no English and that the Italian he had studied for three or four weeks before leaving home proved so inadequate! He remained less than a week, terminated his stay with an emotional display, and returned home. In the meantime his wife determined to leave him, but upon his return he became repentant, promised her to be more responsible in the future, and persuaded her to take him back. One cannot blame her too much, for Joseph is the one colorful experience in an otherwise drab life.

Since that time he has alternately lived with his mother, who is now a widow, and with his wife. At present, at the age of thirty-four, he has decided to become a doctor. Joseph undoubtedly has the mental capacity to enter one of the professions, but he cannot understand that he has an inadequate preparation, that his characterological defects may prevent his success, or that he is too old now to start on such a long program of work. He is at present taking premedical courses in which he does no more than average work. He will never be allowed to enter medical school because his grades are too poor. The money for this study has been paid jointly by his mother and wife, the former out of her meager inheritance from her husband and the latter out of her daily earnings. As Joseph nears the end of his premedical work, he is realizing the impossibility of becoming a doctor. He is beginning to cut his classes and to project the blame on everyone but himself; he is gradually working himself up into a rage, at the height of which he will undoubtedly deliver an emotional blast to the college officials and then withdraw from his classes.

This young man is completely without a sense of duty. His irresponsibility is that of a small child who follows every whim and produces a temper tantrum if circumstances block the fulfillment of his desires.

Finally, an adult is tolerant of those who differ from him in color, creed, nationality, religion, point of view, or social status. Everyone knows supposedly grown-up people who have carried into their adult years the intolerance and snobbishness of adolescence. A boy or girl of sixteen normally condemns those who are in any way different and looks with scorn upon other cliques than that to which he or she belongs, but the persistence of such prejudiced attitudes into adulthood is abnormal and is a clear proof of moral immaturity. The adults who want native-born Japanese deprived of their citizenship are on a par with the high school pupils who want the school dances closed to all foreigners, regardless of their merits as individuals. The white aviator who froths at the mouth because Negroes can now also earn their wings is displaying the same immaturity as those exclusive high school children who resent having a scholarship prize won by the son of a cobbler. The mother who insists upon imposing her small-town social views upon her cosmopolite daughter, the pig-headed religious fanatic, and the rabid labor agitator all show a childish one-sidedness and stubbornness in their thinking. People manage to be intolerant about all kinds of things, as a few examples from everyday life will show.

Mrs. M grew up in the deep south and was educated both to be dependent upon Negro servants and to look down upon all members of the race. She married a northerner and went to live in a New England city. Here she would employ no one but Negroes, although she had great difficulty in getting them to do housework. She stated bluntly that she would not insult any white girl by asking her to do the menial work of a maid. The northern Negroes did not suit her at all, however, and it was rare for her to keep a girl for more than a month. She admitted they did their work but insisted they did not know their place. The housemaid was not allowed to use the same silver or dishes used by the family, she ate different and inferior food cooked in special pans, she had access only to a toilet in the basement, and she had to take sponge baths in her room after carrying a bucket of water there for the purpose. Mrs. M would not trade at a store if it sold things even by mail to Negroes. She would not permit her children to attend public school because there might be a Negro in the room. I have known her to get off a streetcar when a Negro entered it. She never again patronized her favorite hotel after it had entertained the Tuskegee Glee Club. She forbade her son to play football because there was a Negro on the squad, and on one occasion she walked out of a friend's house because the rest of the group turned on the radio to listen to Paul Robeson. To this day Mrs. M has remained obdurate and intolerant. She makes trouble for herself, her family, and her acquaintances by the rigidity of her attitude and by her refusal to accord Negroes their share of human worth, human rights, and human dignity.

Mr. Hudson is a man of about sixty who has been for some years on the relief rolls although he has a record of having been an expert carpenter. He is still in good health and, especially in the present labor shortage, could support himself with repair work in his neighborhood if he were not intolerant of other people's ideas. He will refinish your furniture with expert skill, but when it is done it is not light grey as you instructed him to make it, but golden oak, or mahogany, or whatever other hue he thinks you should be wanting. He will enlarge your study table so skillfully that the joints of the added parts do not show, but when you come to use it you find he has put the shelves where you as a southpaw cannot conveniently get at them, although your directions to him were perfectly clear. If you stand over him and exert the full force of your

MORAL MATURITY

personality, he will paint a wall instead of kalsomining it, but you have to put up with a steady tirade of objections. He is perfectly competent to build a garage, but he will argue for days about where it should be put in an effort to browbeat you into locating it on the spot he thinks appropriate. You can instruct him to build a bookcase in which each successive shelf is shorter than the one below it, but he turns up with a superlatively neat bookcase in which all shelves are the same length and tells you you would be crazy to waste space as you had planned. In short he is a completely intolerant person whose ideas are rigid and unalterable. No one else is ever right. In spite of having failed many times to receive pay for his work because it was not done according to specifications, he continues to enforce his preconceptions upon anyone so misguided as to hire him.

Dolores Selden came to a personnel bureau to ask advice regarding certain misunderstandings which greatly troubled her between her mother and herself. The situation, as I came to know it from interviews with both Dolores and her mother, was so common that it may almost be called typical of the modern home.

Dolores was an attractive, vivacious girl who was decidedly popular with boys. She pursued the usual custom of going with first one boy and then another without concentrating her attention upon anyone, said she knew enough about sex to leave it alone, and seemed innocent of anything more than the usual good times; in short, she appeared generally to be a typical, self-sufficient, modern girl. Her objective, nonsentimental, easygoing boy-and-girl friendships ought to have delighted the heart of any anxious mother. But quite the contrary was the case.

Her mother simply could not understand how Dolores could be so "promiscuous" in selecting her friends. She constantly feared the worst, and seemed quite unconscious of the fact that her daughter was well armored against sex excitement by the sophistication of the modern girl.

The mother deplored modern dancing, would not allow cardplaying in her home, refused permission to her children to attend the movies, scolded constantly about filthy modern novels, and generally made herself incomprehensible to her children. She said she was willing that Dolores have her friends come to the house, but what, Dolores asked frankly, could they do when they got there? By the time Dolores had finished a year of college she and her mother had succeeded in coming to a complete misunderstanding. The mother argued that Dolores should not go out often with a boy unless she intended to marry him. She stated that when *she* was a girl anyone who behaved as Dolores did would be an outcast from nice society, as was probably true. She was sure it was time for her daughter to settle down and find herself a mate before she built up such a reputation for recklessness that no man would want her. The daughter's reply was, of course, that she was just an average girl, that she did nothing wrong, and that her mother was out of date.

The great difficulty about this misunderstanding was that both mother and daughter were right. The mother, talking about conditions of her own girlhood, could not realize that times had changed. Dolores, talking about conditions as she saw them, could not realize that her mother's youth was lived under different circumstances. The mother was trying desperately and sincerely to save her daughter from what she saw as frightful ruin, for she based her interpretation of Dolores' conduct upon the attitudes current in her own girlhood. Dolores was trying to live the active, straightforward, independent, and fundamentally more healthy life of the girl of today, a life in which many young men have a part. If either had been less sincere in her convictions there would have been less trouble.

My own efforts in dealing with this situation were directed primarily toward bringing about some understanding between these excellent representatives of two generations. Several interviews with the mother soon made it clear, however, that she had become so thoroughly conventionalized, so shut in by her prejudices, that it was impossible to bring her to any glimpse of the changes in attitudes and points of view which had taken place since her girlhood. In fact, the very possibility of such changes seemed inconceivable to her; the manners and customs of rural Indiana thirty years ago seemed to her the one inspired, eternally-right-and-never-to-be-questioned mode of life. Dolores, however, soon came to an excellent understanding of the situation. She now tried to explain things whenever possible, to make allowance for differences in point of view, and to conduct herself so as to arouse as little antagonism as possible. It is probable that through her efforts any real disruption will be avoided. But as long as Dolores lives at home she will be subject to chronic criticism and nagging because she insists upon being a normal girl of her generation. Soon she will graduate, obtain a position elsewhere—and proceed to live her own life in her own way.

Dolores' difficulties are those faced by thousands of girls today. Of late years there has been added to the ever-present distrust of one generation for another the confusion and the conflict of attitudes inevitable in a society which is rapidly changing. *A priori*, it would seem that the parent should be the one most likely to have perspective and broad judgment in such a situation, since the parent has seen the change come about. But very often it is the child only who comes to an understanding and who must bear the burden of adjustment if any adjustment is made.

In pleasant contrast to such examples of intolerance triumphant is a recent instance that came to my attention:

Last spring the officials of a large state university were subjected to a good deal of alumni pressure because it became known that the yearly scholarship prize, if given on the usual objective basis, would be won by a Japanese boy, a youngster so brilliant that his major department predicted success and fame for him in no uncertain terms. Some members of the faculty also entered protests and wanted the second-best student, a one hundred per cent American, to receive the prize. The officials, however, were adults who could stand firmly against the absurdly childish pressure to which they were being subjected. The Japanese lad got the prize, but he was not there to receive it, because he was already in an assembly center. As the university's president said in making the award, the "winner's country had need of him elsewhere." This solution was made on the basis of adult tolerance, not adolescent snobbishness.

The true adult treats others as individuals, on the basis of their merits and without respect to the racial, national, or social group to which they belong. Naturally, anyone can make a mistake in his estimates of people, but a mature person does not make the particular mistake of closing his mind to others because of the group from which they come. *What* people are is important; *who* they are is of no consequence.

PART III
Popular Escapes from Maturity

CHAPTER 7

Escape by Fantasy

THE HUMAN MIND is extremely ingenious in finding ways of escape from maturity and reality. I am reminded of the mental fertility shown by lazy students who could get A's if they would apply as much energy and originality to doing their work as they expend in avoiding it. Humanity could look reality in the eye without flinching too much, if it would only stop running in the other direction. Not being equipped with eyes before and behind like the beasts of the Apocalypse, an individual in full flight cannot be expected to see what is back of him.

A person is making a psychological escape whenever he interprets the world as being different from what it is, especially when his interpretation makes it more agreeable to him. Instead of adjusting himself to the realities of life and the requirements of adulthood, the escaper interprets life to suit himself. He lacks the courage to face the world, so he turns his back on it and makes believe it either is not there or is quite different from its actuality. When thus upholstered, reality becomes softer, pleasanter, and easier to cope with. It is therefore not surprising that most people turn escapist some of the time and the more thin-skinned most of the time.

One of the commonest forms of escape and one of the least harmful when indulged in only moderately is the use of fantasy. By this means the escapist imagines both himself and the world as different from the actual situation. The almost universal form of escape by fantasy is the daydream. The undersized clerk with an almost pathological shyness and a hampering feeling of insecurity can imagine himself as the outstanding rookie of the year, as a daring pilot who has been awarded the D.S.C., as a famous scientist with a whole alphabet after his name, as a financier whose deeds make or break the market, or as the cowboy hero of many rodeos. Such imaginings give him release from his own limitations and from those of his environment. As long as he is perfectly clear in his own mind which is real and which is imaginary no harm is done. Neither is any good done, unfortunately. By his fantasies he has escaped reality for a while, but he has changed neither it nor himself. He is still small, timid, and insecure; and the world is still hard, unfriendly, and overpowering. Instead of building up a habit of daydreaming he would react in a more mature way if he were to take objective stock of himself, decide what he might do that would satisfy his drives better than being a clerk, consider how he can either overcome or adjust to his handicaps, and lay out a practical course of action for reaching his goal. He would need to be sure that he was not fooling himself about either his own capabilities or the characteristics of the world about him.

ESCAPE BY FANTASY

Mary Louise at the age of sixteen had just come to the city from a small town. Her mother had recently died and her father thought Mary Louise would get over the shock faster in new surroundings. In the city she lived in the home of distant relatives where her father paid for her room and board. The people with whom she lived were elderly and were much pleased that Mary Louise was unusually quiet and did not bring a lot of noisy young people to the house.

The girl's earlier childhood presents an interesting history. In the first grade she had formed an intense emotional attachment to another girl of her own age. The two became practically inseparable for several years. The other girl was considerably more capable than Mary Louise but was devoted to her. The relationship between the two was more that of a messiah and a disciple than that of equals. Mary Louise's parents had been more than willing for her to be continually with this friend because the other girl came from a family whose social standing and economic level were conspicuously higher than their own. The friendship had continued until Mary Louise was twelve when her friend's family moved to another state. This event precipitated a crisis. From the first grade on Mary Louise had developed no other friendships. After her chum departed she either made no effort to replace her, or else was so inexperienced in social contacts that she did not succeed. Soon Mary Louise began to daydream, inventing scenes in which she and her chum participated. She continued to do reasonably good work in school. Other children had no objection to her. In fact they paid little attention to her one way or another.

When Mary Louise was sixteen she became bored with school and wanted to get a job. Her father thought she would find better openings in the city, so he sent her there and asked his relatives to help her get started in some large firm. After a little job-hunting Mary Louise found a position with a firm that employed more than two thousand workers. Here she was completely lost. She knew no one and she had never learned how to strike up an acquaintance with strangers. The elderly people with whom she lived were too old to furnish much companionship or to have friends who were Mary Louise's age. From being lonely and moody Mary Louise became isolated and profoundly depressed.

After about two years she was recommended for transfer to another department. As a routine measure, she was sent to the personnel office for an interview. The conversation covered a number of topics and from it the following facts emerged. Mary Louise had no complaints in regard to her life except that she was always tired. She had given up trying to understand people or to get along with them. She was resigned to being an unobtrusive shadow in the office and she definitely did not want to take part in social activities. She was out of touch with human relationships. She said she had rather read some interesting book and then think out new episodes with the characters than to be with actual people. Since it took her three or four hours every week-day evening and an entire weekend to get through a book of average length one can assume that she spent more time daydreaming and weaving fantasies around the plot than she did in reading. Mary Louise showed a consistent mood of depression and a fatigue to which she could assign no cause. Most serious in the girl's condition were her resignation to things as they were and her lack of normal drives. She expressed a faint hope that she might someday find another friend like the one she had once had, but otherwise she showed no desire to resume human contacts. That is, she wanted a hero or heroine to worship, and she did not seem to have any conception of more ordinary and mature forms of friendship.

This girl had made an almost perfect escape into fantasy, although remaining sane. The people she read, thought, and dreamed about were already clearer in her mind than those among whom she worked, but she still knew which people were real and which were imaginary. As a person she reminded one of a lost child. Indeed it seemed unlikely that she had matured much since her chum had left her, six years earlier, or that she would mature appreciably for some time to come. She was not developing out of her childishness because her daydreams formed a buffer between her and the realities of life.

Other types of escape by fantasy are less obvious than the compensatory daydream. A few samples taken at random would include: the woman who thinks the world is not especially harsh but that, since she is so extraordinarily sensitive and fine, she must suffer in proportion to her fastidiousness; the trusting soul who believes blindly that everything is for the best, that all people are good and that God will care for His own; the man who looks with scorn and derision upon most people as being his inferiors in ability and explains his own lack of material progress by thinking the world is against him; the recluse who loses himself in ideas and books to such an extent that he does not remember the outside world; the gangster who is convinced that every person in the world hates every other and would not hesitate to kill if there were an advantage in it for himself; the fanatic who thinks that he and those who agree with him are headed for heaven and everyone else straight for hell; the smart-aleck who thinks the whole world is a joke; the person who believes that every man is the competitor of every other man and that life is a never-ending struggle for superiority; the poet or artist who sees only beauty and will not so much as look at ugliness; the patient soul who is certain that in this world each one will be rewarded according to his deserts. The list could be prolonged almost indefinitely to show the different attitudes that people develop to protect themselves. In all cases, the individual has seized upon one aspect of reality, magnified it, distorted it, and disregarded all others. Thus one person sees kindliness about him and thinks the world is one hundred per cent kind, while another sees cruelty about him and thinks the world one hundred per cent cruel. The whole business of misinterpretation reminds one of the poem about the seven blind men and the elephant in which one of them who touched the tail said an elephant was like a rope, while another who touched the ear said an elephant was like a fan, and a third who touched the side said an elephant was like a wall, and so on. Each one believed he held the whole of reality when he held only a piece of it. In a similar manner people fool themselves by their fantasies and misconceptions about the world.

When carried to an extreme fantasy is dangerous because the dreamer eventually fails to distinguish between his dreams and the world about him. When a person reaches this stage of confusion he is insane. A lunatic will dash himself screaming against doors and windows when he merely thinks his house is on fire, while he may allow himself to be burned to a cinder when it is actually ablaze, because to him reality lies in the world created by his thoughts. Many a mediaeval monk reached this state of absorption in fantasy, when his visions of heaven and the angels became real to him and he did not notice that he was emaciated, ragged, and dirty, or that other people than himself so much as existed.

It should be noticed that the type of fantasy here described is in the main an uncontrolled and unconstructive exercise of the imagination. Its function is to give an outlet to some repression or maladjustment. The daydreamer's mind idles along, giving satisfaction to submerged emotions but without direction toward either the artistic expression of the dreamer's mood or the solution of practical problems. The poet, the playwright, the artist, the musician, the inventor, the scientist, the mathematician, and the philosopher all use their imaginations but their dreams are constructive and their imaginative reactions are directed toward an end. The artist has something to say through whatever medium he selects, and the scientist has a problem to solve. Both may use fantasy and most certainly both are imaginative, but they do not indulge in aimless daydreaming. Perhaps the best way to express the difference between them and the type of reaction described in this chapter is to say that the scientist and the artist and the philosopher use their imaginations for a purpose—whether conscious or unconscious—not to escape anything; that is, they are running towards whatever problems preoccupy their interest, whereas the daydreamer is running away from his.

Although extremes of fantasy are obviously unhealthy, many psychologists feel that a little distortion here and there provides a useful and harmless outlet. This point of view is based upon the assumption that not even a mature person can possibly stand reality and must therefore have some form of escape from it. If this assumption is true then a mild degree of fantasy and a slight rearrangement of the world to make it pleasanter, is probably as harmless as any other form of avoiding the truth. The main objection is that even a minor distortion of reality gives one the habit of escape and makes an objective and candid estimate of the world more difficult than ever. An occasional vivid daydream perhaps does no more than to turn one partly away from the world, thus producing a view of reality as glimpsed from the corner of one eye. The slight distortion produced from this angle is better than the complete blindness of one whose back is turned, but the full front view is a lot better, assuming that one can stand it.

Sometimes the fantasies appear only indirectly in a person's behavior and involve a misinterpretation of his or her capabilities or characteristics. The people who exaggerate, or tell smallish lies in order to make a story more interesting, or quote what others did not say are often daydreamers who have entirely misinterpreted themselves and their position among their peers. In their fantasies they regard themselves as popular, sought after, admired; in reality they are usually unpopular, avoided, looked down upon. Such a situation is so hard to accept that one must either grow up sufficiently to alter it or else seek comfort for one's ego by escape. The underlying inferiorities that have produced the situation often yield to proper treatment but not until after one is willing to stop running away and becomes sufficiently mature to separate facts from fables.

One of my childhood friends is an excellent example of unintentional malingering and misinterpretation of both herself and her environment.

Whenever I see her, at intervals ranging from three to ten years, she dilates at length about the wonderful times she had when she lived in M-----, the place where I first knew her. She reminisces about what a lovely group of friends she went around with and what fun she had, all in contrast to the isolation she feels at present. My recollection of the situation is quite different. She was a fat and rather sloppy-looking girl whom most of us avoided assiduously, and if she had such wonderful times I don't know why she should have complained to me so bitterly and constantly of how unhappy she was. I do not doubt that her childhood days contained some pleasant experiences, but most of those I recall were on the unpleasant side from her point of view. Yet this woman looks back to her childhood as a golden age. She has covered the memory of her early years with such a thick veil of fancy and sentiment that she no longer recalls what actually happened. Indeed she had woven into her childhood saga a number of events that I feel reasonably certain she got out of some book, since neither I nor others who knew her as a child have the faintest recollection of them. If her retroactive fantasies seem to soften life for her, who am I to deny her the comfort of a little harmless malingering? The fact remains, however, that the difference between truth and fancy eludes her whenever she recalls her earlier years.

The efforts of another young woman to achieve objective maturity in her estimates of herself illustrate a second kind of escape into fantasy, the resulting misinterpretation of the self, the social maladjustment, and the eventual growing up into an ability to face herself without the protection of the traits she had in imagination assigned to herself.

Dorine was a young woman of twenty-two who worked as saleslady in a fashionable dress shop. She lived at the Y.W.C.A., where she had made herself conspicuous by adopting mannerisms, posing, and availing herself of every opportunity to attract attention. As a result she had lost the respect and good will of other girls and women both in the shop and in the Y.W.C.A. Her efforts to attract attention had led her into such exhibitionistic and dramatic reactions as keeping first a chameleon, then a garter snake, and finally two toads in her room, to the consternation of the other residents of the dormitory. After a while she attempted something slightly more sophisticated, namely announcing her engagement to an aviator whose name had recently been in the papers. No one believed her, but she continued to tell tall stories of how men pestered her with attentions or sought her out at parties or drove four hundred miles just to be with her for an hour or two. By all this self-proffered evidence she showed her concept of herself as a popular young woman.

When this method of impressing herself upon others failed to work she resorted to another bit of self-delusion. She became the suffering and misunderstood heroine. In this phase, which is a bit less childish than the earlier one, she told people all about herself and her fancied problems, going into great detail and apparently seeking their advice. She seized with avidity upon each new acquaintance and proceeded to pour out her soul all over again. It had soon become clear, however, that she was merely working for attention, for she talked much too fluently and easily for her troubles to be real and gave little heed to the advice she received. The suffering act did not go over any better than the success story. Eventually Dorine developed a third concept of herself. This time she was the young dreamer, unhappy and melancholy almost to the point of suicide. She wore a gloomy expression, talked little, ate little, at least in public, wore black, sat staring at the wall, and went on lonely walks in the rain. This act really alarmed her acquaintances.

At this point a middle-aged psychologist happened to move into the Y.W.C.A. The girls were not long in asking her to take a look at Dorine and see if something could not be done to help her in overcoming her unpleasant desire for attention. The psychologist therefore went out of her way to talk to Dorine and eventually succeeded in analyzing the girl's difficulties and bringing about a partial readjustment.

Dorine had been an only child and a very spoiled one. Her parents lavished love, attention, and money upon her. In 1931 her father shot himself because his fortune had been wiped out, and her mother died soon after. Enough money was saved from the crash to board Dorine with a neighbor while she finished high school but then she had to find a job. The change from being the center of an admiring family to being one salesgirl among many was more than her ego could bear. She therefore took refuge in misinterpretations of herself—first as a popular person, then as an individual bearing up bravely under trouble, and finally as one crushed by melancholy.

Dorine was at bottom no such fool as she appeared on the surface. She grasped quite well the childishness of her reactions and the reasons for them. She admitted her urge to be regarded as the most important person in her immediate circle, but she eventually saw that the only way to appear important was to *be* important and that all substitutes were easily detected shams. She finally realized that she was just an ordinary girl whose chief assets were a normal mind, an ease in meeting people, and a good deal of ambition. She was advised to take courses in salesmanship and did so, with a resulting advancement in her work. She kept a strict watch over her tendency to lie and tried hard to be her natural self. In a year's time she became head of a small department with two clerks under her. This position, plus the real affection her reformation produced among the girls with whom she lived, gave her sufficient satisfaction to inhibit further distortions of herself in fantasy. Ten years have now passed. Dorine is head buyer of a large firm but, more important, she has accepted her real self and has matured into a likable person.

Escape into fantasy may thus consist of a misinterpretation of the world in some way that will make facing it a relatively easy task, or of a misinterpretation of one's self that will conceal unpleasant truth and flatter one's ego. Both reactions are equally fatal to maturity, because people grow up by overcoming difficulties, not by running away from them and living behind a thick fog of make-believe.

CHAPTER 8

Escape by Play

IN THIS connection, the word "play" is used to mean all escapes through viewing the world lightly, superficially, humorously, or jokingly, as well as escape through overt play. This latter form is open only to the wealthy. Most of us are mercifully saved from it by the necessity of earning a living. The rich young man who follows the sun from Florida to Maine and back again every year with a season in New York, is commonly and accurately described as a playboy. He swims, plays tennis or golf, attends the races, watches sundry sports, drinks and flirts more or less, dances, makes a play for the more popular debutantes, loafs in the sun, gets married and divorced occasionally, and generally turns life into a continuous game. In the end he gets punished by his own aimlessness and boredom, but to many people tied to a job his existence looks like the answer to prayer. He and his feminine counterpart are avoiding reality as completely as possible and have substituted for it a play world in which the one objective is to have fun. The immaturity of such behavior is too obvious to need elaboration. Play may be the chief occupation of a small child but certainly not of a grown man or woman.

Less overt forms of escape by play are more common though less conspicuous. To some escapists life is a joke, and everyone and everything is funny. I do not mean that humor is an undesirable reaction or that no amusement is to be derived from the world and the people in it. Those sober souls who see nothing funny in life are to be pitied, because life will almost certainly become too heavy for them to bear. The type of escapist to whom I refer is a person who finds all things funny, regardless of their importance or seriousness. One such individual dashed up to me recently and exclaimed, "You know how M always fussed about her husband's drinking! Well, she ought to be happy now! He won't drink any more. He died in his sleep last night." To this man death had no dignity and bereavement no pathos; presumably, he could bear neither, so he made a joke of them.

Another acquaintance has been for more than forty years the self-appointed humorist of a certain college campus. All day long every day her wit played over whatever came to her attention. The students were usually entranced when they first met her because she made them laugh, but after a while they got either bored with or annoyed by the persistence and irrelevancy of her humor. It was almost impossible to get from her a sensible answer to a sensible question. Her colleagues distrusted her because her view of the world was so superficial and warped. She never cared who got hurt by what she said, and on one occasion became furious with me because I told her that remarks which hurt others were often tremendously clever but never funny. She dislikes violently other persons with so much as a glimmer of wit—like most humorists she wants admirers not competitors—and she selects for her intimates those who are utterly without humor of their own. After some forty-eight years of hourly use her gaiety is wearing thin, and she is discovering at long last that age, disease, and unpopularity are things at which she dare not laugh. Her merry but superficial attitude toward life has become a poor thing to lean upon. An unhappier person or one less ready to face the inevitable ravages of senescence, I do not know.

Laughter may be either release or defense. When it is a reaction to the minor foibles of humanity or the incidental inanities of the world it is usually a helpful release. Professional humorists, on the other hand, use their wit to conceal their seriousness and to keep you and me from noticing it. They do not think life a joke and they use humor as a defense. But when an overdeveloped sense of humor keeps one from seeing the world in its true proportions, it is no less an escape than any daydream.

Sooner or later, the humorist meets something he cannot laugh off and then he makes the sad discovery that he has neither the courage nor the maturity for facing life. "Laugh, clown, laugh" is a fine motto as long as the clown is still able to laugh, but when his merriment fails he has nothing left. Once reality has torn a hole in the bright veil of his gaiety and he gets an unclouded view of reality, he discovers he is poorly prepared to face a life that is no joke at all.

Escape into play, either actually or emotionally, is as unsound as any other escape. Moreover it leads to deadly boredom. Skittering about upon the surface of life may be amusing for a while, but it palls eventually. It produces a diet of all cake and no bread; if, as the Good Book says, man cannot live by bread alone, he is surely much less able to survive exclusively on cake.

CHAPTER 9

Escape by Solitude

THERE are times when most people find the world too much with them and therefore seek solitude for a while, but they soon get lonely and return to circulation voluntarily. To them solitude is only a respite from overstrain, not an escape, and as such it is healthy and beneficial. The true escapist goes into permanent solitude, turns his back on the world, narrows his activities to those for which he needs no assistance from others, and resigns himself to loneliness. The motives for this behavior are many, but the loss of contact with reality and the failure to reach full maturity are inevitable. Usually the escapist has suffered some unfortunate experiences in his youthful efforts to find his place in the world and has as a consequence decided that the common herd is beneath his notice, or that the world is a nasty place, or that life is too complex for a person of his singular and commendable simplicity. In any case he pretends either that the world does not exist outside his own slight contacts with it or, if he grant it recognition at all, that it is of no importance. The recluse who lives in an ivory tower of his own making is a fairly common phenomenon.

Some fifty years ago a young man was trying hard to progress in a certain business firm. Unfortunately he was of inferior ability, which he tried to conceal behind a cloak of arrogance and boorishness. He was unpopular with his agemates, but he had a usefulness to the firm in handling bookkeeping details on certain small accounts. The head of his department gave him a tiny office by himself and left him alone. After fifty years he is still there and still handling the same details. He comes and goes in silence, will not return a greeting, writes letters to his immediate superior whenever communication is necessary instead of talking to him, lives in the same rented room he first occupied thirty years ago, brings home his meals in a paper bag and eats them alone, spends his spare time in reading medieval history, and has not been known to have so much as an acquaintance for many years. In disposition he is querulous, contentious, disagreeable, suspicious, and mean. He has only scorn and derision toward others. If some kind person tries to be agreeable to him, he becomes suspicious and avoids further contact. His entire concept of the world is that it is unjust, dishonest, deceitful, intolerant, and downright wicked, while the human race is on a par with a particularly aggressive and tricky rattlesnake. His escape into solitude is complete. Aside from the trifling clerical assistance to his firm, his life is useless even to himself.

Roscoe was an extremely precocious child. At the age of five, when I first knew him, he was already reading such books as *Treasure Island* or *Huckleberry Finn*. When he entered school he was put at once into the third grade and half a year later, just after his sixth birthday, he was advanced to the fourth. He still had plenty of leisure, which he employed in learning Latin. By the time he was eight he had advanced to the seventh grade and was reading Cicero in the original during his spare time. The neighborhood children had no comprehension whatever of him so they looked down upon him, teased him unmercifully, bullied him more or less, and ignored his tentative efforts to be friendly. Roscoe graduated from the ninth grade at the age of ten, only to find that the high school would not accept him. He therefore went to a private tutor who introduced him to what has turned into the passion of his life, Greek. Since the normal children of the neighborhood would pay no attention to him, Roscoe used to spend hours reading and explaining passages in Greek to an imbecile girl who was so defective she never went to school. Roscoe was the only person who was really nice to her, and she rewarded him by listening quietly and smiling pleasantly while he read Greek aloud. She would not have understood the passages any better in English.

In the course of time Roscoe passed as a shadow through high school and college. It is doubtful if the other pupils knew he was there. He took no part in any activity, he made no acquaintances—even his teachers could establish little contact with him although his work was always excellent. When not in class he was at home poring over Greek writers. The only person with whom he could relax and talk was his former tutor, now a blind, feeble old man. In college Roscoe made Phi Beta Kappa but no friends.

He is now a professor of Greek and an eminent classical scholar, but he is still an immature and naive person to whom many childish oddities of behavior continue to cling. He mutters to himself, he cringes when he hears someone laugh unexpectedly, he is afraid of strangers, he keeps his eyes on the ground so that he will not have to speak to acquaintances who may perhaps cut him dead, he slips about the campus like a ghost, and he avoids his students of whom he is much afraid. Roscoe has never shown an overt interest in girls or indeed any sexual interests at all. He is a normal person albeit a very childish one, except in intellectual matters. I find him quite delightful; he relaxes with me into his most normal behavior, probably because I never threw rocks at him in his childhood and because he knows I do not mind being subjected to a scholarly harangue on the minutiae of Homeric verb forms. To me

Roscoe is still a frightened and bewildered small boy, but I can see that others might think him more than a little odd. As the years pass the student saga about his mannerisms, habits, and queer sayings grows longer while he continues to live on his desert island with long-dead Greeks for company.

One young man of my acquaintance is well on his way to his particular ivory tower. About five years ago, in a passion of youthful revolt, he left home and indignantly spurned further help from his parents. For some months he wandered about the country living a hand-to-mouth existence until he fell into one more casual job that turned out to be something fascinating. He was hired along with several other sturdy young men to help dig up archaeological specimens. For the first time in his life he became interested in ideas. Something about the immensity of time as witnessed by these relics of prehistoric man seemed to thrill him. The head of the expedition encouraged him to develop his interest. The young man went on several trips with his mentor, and in between trips he took courses in archaeology, some by correspondence, at sundry universities. At present he cares for nothing but the archaeology of Southern Colorado and refuses to get a college degree because he would have to study other subjects. Since he is young and personally presentable he has several friends and acquaintances in his home town, but he leaves them instantly and without regret whenever he has a chance to dig. His entire world consists of a space in Colorado some two hundred miles square, and he has no real respect for the millions of people in the world to whom his consuming passion is of no moment. A few weeks ago he was called on the draft, but the draft board wisely classified him as 4F, in spite of his splendid physique and excellent health. He is already so withdrawn from the world that he is useless in practical situations. In another five years he will not know that anything outside his narrow interests so much as exists. He may become an outstanding local archaeologist for he has a good grasp of his specialty, but he will never be a normal human being unless he stops ignoring all but one small fragment of reality.

Mrs. LeBosquet is a widow of almost sixty who has not left her house and grounds for well over twenty years. Sometimes she remains for weeks at a time in one or two rooms. Part of her expenses are paid by her children and part of them she earns by making lace, crocheting, knitting, and embroidering. Her work is so exquisite and brings such a good price that the various shops through which she takes orders are willing to send messengers to bring her materials and collect her finished work. Mrs. LeBosquet is by no means unsociable. Her friends and neighbors are constantly in and out of the house, she holds long telephone conversations, and she is an incorrigible letter writer. She reads newspapers and magazines, keeps up to date, and is a lively and interesting person. There is nothing of the recluse in her manner. In every way she seems a well-adjusted person except that she will not leave her house.

If Mrs. LeBosquet's conduct is the result of an inner conflict, its emotional content has certainly been lost for a long time, for she is as serene and restful as anyone I know. Her behavior has seemed to me to be a flight from the world rather than a reaction to any specific problem or situation, especially in view of her history. She is a peasant from the south of France, a rather simply organized person from a relatively simple environment. Cosmopolitan New York was probably too much for her; she lived on the East Side for a few years, of which she rarely speaks. From there she went into permanent seclusion in a small city at no great distance. In her home and garden she made for herself a life she could understand, a life that had meaning for her. As the years passed her children grew up, married, and went away. She made no move to stop them, and indeed always encouraged them to live average lives. If her choice for herself were, as I suspect, between an imperfect and strained adaptation to modern life and a withdrawal to an environment to which she could adjust easily and happily, who can say that she chose the poorer alternative? Her reaction has been a regression, but it is happier than the severe neurosis she might have developed. Perhaps for an immigrant girl from a rural background who was ill-equipped for metropolitan life she has done well to find peace, even at the cost of a flight into solitude.

Escape into solitude is usually so unhealthy that its disadvantages require no emphasizing. It is also an immature solution to the problems of life. The social isolationist is showing the same behavior as that of the small child who gets mad at the way a game is being played, retires to the sidelines in a huff, jeers at his playmates for a while, and eventually wanders off by himself, frightened and alone. Fortunately most people are too sociable to have much taste for solitude and too mature to sacrifice themselves rather than compromise. Other people may be annoying at times but with all their faults they are better than no one at all.

CHAPTER 10

Escape by Fanaticism

THE FANATIC is a common enough phenomenon, but few people stop to think how lopsided his notions of reality are. He sees life from one angle only and succeeds in remaining immune to any notion that does not prove him to be right. Thus the religious fanatic may see the world as a sink of iniquity; in the daily newspaper he finds much to back up this attitude, but he fails to notice the items that contradict it. He may think all women are prostitutes just because some of them are. He probably does not set out to distort reality, but he picks out from what he sees and hears only those items that reinforce his fanaticism, and consequently his view of the world is one-sided, immature, and colored with his own bias.

I know an otherwise sensible enough man who has become convinced that the only good Japanese are dead ones. He wants all Japanese sent back to Japan and a future ban to be set against further immigration. In the meantime, the country should treat them as badly as possible. He will not admit that a decent, loyal Japanese exists. In his view all of them take their orders straight from the Emperor and, if allowed loose in a community, would murder us all in our beds. He does not pay any attention to the obvious fact that between Pearl Harbor and May 20 of the next year, when all Japanese in the San Francisco Bay area were evacuated, no one was molested by them. He relates remarks and stories to prove his point, but will usually not even listen when another person presents similar data to contradict him. If he listens at all it is with an air of condescension which says more clearly than words that those who defend aliens may be sincere but they are most terribly stupid in their failure to see through the situation as he does. It would be hard to find his equal for sheer stubborn childishness.

By adopting fanaticism this man avoids the necessity for further thought and escapes from the many contradictions that grate upon the person who prefers taking facts as they come. It requires hard work to keep an open mind and to go through the process of changing it as fresh evidence appears. Reality is generally confusing and contradictory; in its many-sidedness it can bewilder and terrify anyone who does not have the courage, the industry, the emotional equilibrium, and the intelligence to observe its many strands and to sort them out. It is easier to make up one's mind, preferably in advance of any objective evidence at all, and then to attend only to those stimuli that reinforce the conclusion already reached on the basis of prejudice. Fanaticism is thus a flight from reality, an unwillingness to face the complexities of life, an erection of an incorrect but harmonious world in which everything hangs together. It is a particularly vicious form of escape because, once begun, it becomes its own defense against the invasion of new ideas and thus gradually encloses the escapist in a hermetically sealed mental chamber where he is doomed to remain. He succeeds therefore in escaping from confusion at the cost of spending his life in an emotional and mental strait-jacket.

Herbert came to a state university from a denominational private school in the South. This latter school is maintained by one of the fundamentalist denominations, and most of its students are recruited from the backwoods by means of scholarship contests. Until his eighteenth year Herbert had lived at home on the farm, attending country school about six months a year. In this school he had been an industrious student of rather more than average capacity. He had added to his scant training by reading such books as he could get hold of—mostly English classics and books on religious topics. When he was eighteen he won a scholarship and spent two years in a small denominational college enrolling two hundred pupils and situated in a small town. At the age of twenty he entered the state university in the freshman class, with the intention of becoming a minister.

The university was situated in a modern city of about 500,000. It took Herbert several days to find his way around and he never became accustomed to the noise and bustle. He had never seen traffic lights; he had never ridden in an electric car; he had never bought a meal in a public restaurant. For the first month Herbert was in a daze because of the complete change in environment. At the university he enrolled in freshman classes in English literature, zoology, and psychology. In the English literature course he read samples from both classics and modern writings. It seemed to him the actions of many characters were not condemned nearly enough, while the modern novels struck him as immoral and indecent. In the psychology class he was at first simply bewildered but later became profoundly distressed because the instructor paid no attention to the soul. He frequently interrupted the lectures to ask questions in regard to free will, the power of God, the existence of a conscience, or some other religious matter.

But it was the zoology class that really angered him. The stress was naturally upon the doctrine of evolution, which outraged every belief Herbert had previously been taught. After about a month he stayed after class one day and read the instructor quite a riot act, accusing him of contaminating youth, of teaching false doctrines, and of being an atheist. The instructor, sensing the young man's sincerity, tried to present arguments in his own behalf, but Herbert only threw his textbook on the table and stalked out of the room; he never attended that class again.

At the end of his first semester he failed his work in zoology from nonattendance and his work in English because in his examinations he insisted upon debating points of morality instead of answering the questions. These failures put him on probation. He was sent to the Dean of his college by one of his second-semester teachers who felt herself unable to cope with the boy's problems. The Dean and two members of the psychology department all took turns in trying to argue Herbert out of his fanatic viewpoints, but to no avail. In the middle of the second semester, Herbert wrote a scathing denunciation of the university, sent it to all the administrative officers and to such members of the faculty as he knew, as well as to several editors who, however, knew too much about libel laws to print it. Having delivered this blast, Herbert packed his trunk and went back to his home with the determination later on of attending some theological school where he would find the teaching less irritating to his convictions.

Mrs. B is the terror of the neighborhood. She is probably about seventy years old, a termagant, a crank, a nuisance, and a paranoiac. She constantly calls the police with complaints: radios are too loud—a point on which I agree with her—a lawn-mower is being run too early, a neighbor's small boy thumbed his nose at her, the lid is off someone's garbage pail, a garage door is banging in the wind, and so *ad infinitum*. The police make half-hearted and apologetic calls around the neighborhood and people usually swallow most of their annoyance because they assume Mrs. B is not entirely right in her mind. Actually her mind is clear enough but her attitudes are both peculiar and offensive. One day I saw her going up the rather long flight of steps to her house and noticed that she dropped her purse. She went right in without missing it so I picked it up and carried it to her door. She had not yet had time to get more than a few steps from the entrance and at my ring she popped her head out and said "Go 'way! I never buy anything from peddlers," and slammed the door. Her purse wouldn't go through the letter-slot so I rang again, got my foot in the door, and returned her purse before she could begin a tirade. As I retreated down the steps she called after me to wait. I stood there while she dumped the contents of her purse onto a table and examined everything, finally saying to me, "Well, it's all here. You can go." This episode gives a fair sample of her ordinary behavior. Mrs. B lives alone, having long since alienated her husband and children; she has no visitors or friends, and she is shunned by her neighbors. Workmen will not go to her house, and even the delivery men will not go nearer to her than halfway up the back walk, where they dump their packages and flee. In all matters great and small Mrs. B is as determined to have her own way as a small child and she has fled into utter solitude rather than grow up and learn to compromise. She is not committably insane, but after a few more years of self-centered and lonely rattling about in an empty house, she certainly should be.

Mr. Y was a brilliant young man who taught German. In a somewhat gloomy Byronic way he was handsome, but the petulant, sulky expression of a thoroughly unhappy person rather marred the effect. One felt almost at once that Mr. Y "smoldered" and might explode at any moment. He began his remarks on the first day by telling us that he was wasting his time teaching a beginning class. He assured us we would never learn German and went on to explain how insular Americans were in regard to foreign languages. After about fifteen minutes in this vein he brought up what proved to be his favorite subject—the failure of the institution to segregate its students, with the result that the few able ones were lost in a crowd of nincompoops. He gave us illustrations of how he—in his rather recent undergraduate days at the same institution—had been overlooked by his teachers because he was surrounded by so much mediocrity. Throughout the semester Mr. Y complained steadily. He told us about sundry departmental wranglings and went in detail into what attitude he had taken, why he was right, and what insidious influences were almost certainly to overcome the righteousness of his side in the dispute. In the actual presentation of classwork Mr. Y was quite good, except that he was always argumentative and—in an impersonal sort of way—entirely pessimistic as to our probable work in German. About the middle of the semester Mr. Y began to dictate a few sentences in German at the beginning of each hour. It happened that we had in the group one boy whose parents spoke the language at home. One day this lad challenged Mr. Y's pronunciation of some word on the grounds that Mr. Y had spoken it with a slightly Yiddish accent. This comment may or may not have been justified, but the results were magnificent. Mr. Y expelled the boy from the class then and there and proceeded to spend the remaining part of the hour in telling us how the Jews had been persecuted for centuries and how his superiors had discriminated against him because he was Jewish. It occurred to me that Mr. Y was precisely the type of Jew for whom the Wailing Wall was devised; if he could have wailed there instead of in class he might have been more successful. In disposition he was melancholy, sensitive, suspicious, and insecure; these traits he could perhaps not help having, but he did not have to pass his own difficulties and disappointments on to his students. As it was, students and colleagues alike were annoyed with his emotional attitudes, bored by his complaints, and hesitant about trusting him because no one knew where his prejudices might lead him.

Mr. Y lasted as a teacher for three years at his alma mater, where he had been a phenomenally good student, but he could not obtain a permanent position. He is now doing translations for a museum—a sad, oldish man with a permanent grouch.

Bessie May was the only child of two rather unusual parents. The mother had always been somewhat delicate, but after the birth of her daughter she became a nervous invalid, primarily because she did not want to have any more children and did not have the courage to say as much. She therefore remained for the rest of her rather long life just sick enough to fend off any possible advances from her husband but not sick enough to be without authority in family affairs. The father, being thus rejected by his wife, concentrated his deepest love upon his small daughter. At the same time he had numerous mistresses, although he kept their existence well hidden. The home life of these three people was full of evasions, suppressions, and tension. Bessie May's mother was constantly admonishing her to be careful and especially to be careful of men and boys. The precise harm that might be done her was not clearly explained, but the girl was brought up in a vague fear of unknown males. Her father had from early childhood talked with Bessie May as if she were his equal in age. As she grew into adolescence he worked with her on small research problems that interested them both. In every way he tried to develop her mental capacities, which were well above average to start with. By the middle of her adolescent years Bessie May had a phobia of boys and the intellectual interests of a thirty-year-old woman. It is no wonder that her classmates found her unintelligible. She looked down to some extent upon the girls and had only derision for the boys. It happened that Bessie May had inherited from her mother a certain fragile beauty that made most boys want to protect her. Indeed nature had intended the girl to be soft, cuddly, and appealing, but her father's education had given her great intellectual maturity and self-confidence; it would have been hard to find a girl less in need of protection. Boys were drawn to her because of her looks, but she snubbed them unmercifully. As she grew older her wariness and suspicion toward boys turned into dislike, then into resentment, and finally into a lifelong hatred of men. She became an ardent feminist, largely because of her jealousy of men's personal freedom, plus her resentment against the traditional restrictions of womanhood. Somewhat to the bewilderment of her family she went to a distant women's college rather than to the state university. Upon her arrival there she promptly changed her name from Bessie May to Bernard—a surface indication of her attitude. She went through college at top speed, concentrating exclusively upon acquiring as much learning as possible. Then she went on to graduate school, where she competed with men so successfully as to win a three-year foreign scholarship. Upon her return she entered university teaching where she has been ever since.

She is now over forty—distinguished, highly intelligent, and beautiful to look upon. She rose through the ranks to the headship of her department as rapidly as any man on the faculty. Her colleagues, especially her male colleagues, respect but fear her. This woman's attitude toward men is compounded of the fear taught her by her mother, of her mental superiority to the boys she knew in high school, of her admiration for successful women, of the jealous competition of her graduate and professional years; these components have produced a fanatic feminist and man-hater. She keeps her male acquaintances in a continual state of the jitters. Her beauty attracts them, but she becomes acutely disgusted if they make the slightest advances. There is now little chance that she will change her fundamental attitudes. She will presumably remain a competitor with men and a man-hater all of her life.

These fanatics distorted the world by concentrating upon a single aspect of reality—Herbert upon religious bigotry, Mrs. B upon her extreme distrust of all human beings, Mr. Y upon racial injustice, and Bessie May upon feminism. Their one-sided and inflexible view of reality has kept them immature as well as more or less disagreeable. Nor is there much hope of maturity for them because each has become enclosed in his own system of thought. If one offers them arguments that would be likely to convince a person with an open mind, they produce the kind of tortuous defense that Herr Goebbels evolves to prove that the German débâcle in the Caucasus is a great victory for the unbeatable Nordics. Fanatics use their delusions as buffers against reality, and behind this bulwark they remain children all their lives.

CHAPTER II

Escape by Projection

IN PSYCHOLOGICAL parlance a person is using the mechanism of projection when he escapes from emotional tension by unconsciously transferring the blame for his own shortcomings and failures to someone or something else. Thus the careless workman blames the dullness of his tools, the failing student blames the unfairness of the examination, the man who does not merit a raise blames the prejudice of his foreman, and the tramp by the roadside blames the selfishness and oppression of the rich. By such convenient projections of responsibility the failure avoids discomfort and shame, because he has passed the emotional buck to someone else. As a release from the incidental tensions of life, projection is comfortable and relatively harmless, but as a generalized pattern of existence it is infantile. One evidence of maturity is the ability to accept the consequences of one's behavior. The person who escapes by projection not only refuses to accept this responsibility but also absolves himself of emotional discomfort by blaming others. That the entire process is unconscious does not prevent it from being effectual.

Sometimes the recipient of the projected blame is

a person in the escapist's immediate neighborhood, sometimes it is someone of whom he has read in the newspapers; other escapists may blame historical characters, or impersonal forces, or general circumstances, or particular objects. A man with a bad temper may blame jointly his heredity—on the grounds that his father had a similar choleric disposition—and his mother—on the grounds that she never gave him adequate discipline. When an outburst leads him into the loss of a good job or the alienation of a friend he produces his well-worn excuse to show that he is not to blame. The notion that he could learn to control his temper either does not occur to him or is rejected, probably because control requires a maturity he does not have. Another man may blame the poverty of his early life for all his subsequent difficulties; by this attitude he avoids the need for growing up and admitting that he has done nothing to compensate for his former privations.

Mr. S is a man of about sixty who has what in professorial lingo is generally described as a B+ mind. That is, his intellectual capacity is definitely superior to the average and even shows some slight evidence of originality, but he lacks that extra independence and daring and flair for novelty that is the exclusive possession of the A+ mind. By profession Mr. S is an inventor, and a good one, but he is profoundly unhappy although he has already earned for himself a modest niche in the history of American invention. With this he is not content. He wants to be Edison. He is not satisfied with being comparatively good, but wants to be superlatively best, and for this he lacks the capacity. Toward his many minor contributions he shows only contempt. He cannot reconcile himself to the fact obvious by now to everyone else that he is a good second-rater, and he cannot take refuge in the truth that men like him are enormously valuable to society. A genius does not carry to completion half the good ideas that he propounds during his lifetime, and much of his work would be lost if the B+ minds of the world did not take his suggestions, work over them, add to them, and put them into usable and practical form. In addition they do make contributions of their own, but these are not usually dramatic or profound. Thus Mr. S has twice made a small but vital invention that permitted the concepts of a more capable man to be used, but with such a role he has not been content.

As the years have rolled on he has with increasing frequency projected the blame on to others for the discrepancy between his ambitions and his achievements. His superiors are unfair to him, he lacks facilities, other men steal his ideas, he does not get his share of research funds, his employers give him only hack work. He blames his parents for not sending him to engineering college, although his two years in trade school were made possible only by years of depriving themselves; he even blames his father for having married a poor woman when he could have married a rich widow. He criticizes his own wife for spending too much money, although to others her household expenses seem small, and he skimps on the education of his children. For fully forty-five out of his sixty years he has mercilessly cudgeled his superior, but not superior enough, mind to make it produce the dramatic and bold invention that will make his name a byword throughout the country, and he is profoundly unhappy because he has failed. He has never faced the reality of his shortcomings. Instead, he has projected the blame onto others.

Mrs. L is doubtless classified in the census as a housewife although she still fancies herself as a composer. When I first knew her she was a rather fragile, sensitive, moody girl of sixteen who composed slight snatches of song from

ESCAPE BY PROJECTION

time to time. Her music teachers rated her as having a high grade of musical ability and foretold a successful career for her. In her first year in a conservatory, however, she eloped with an earnest young minister and left for missionary work in India. When I next saw her she was a woman of forty with six children and a settled attitude of discontent. She had had little time for music, and her critical judgment told her that what composing she had done was not first-rate.

In the years since her return from India she has been trying to recapture the spark of genius she probably had once, and she has written one or two things of some merit. Such minor success has, however, been achieved at the cost of neglecting her home and children. She has recently realized that her children, for whom she sacrificed her career, are turning out badly. The oldest girl is a weak, sickly, colorless person, the product of assorted germs that thrive in overpopulated and unsanitary countries. Her mother had not known how to protect her first-born from infection, although she did better with the subsequent children. The oldest boy is not wicked; he is just a loafer and sponger. The second boy already has a juvenile court record and seems headed for worse. The third has quite a bit of musical ability, but he is irresponsible, bad-tempered, and egotistical. The two little girls seem normal enough, and one of them is very bright, but they need more maternal attention than they get.

Mrs. L blames her husband for his inability to earn enough money to support his family better, although one would suppose that she must have known about the chronically impecunious state of ministers before she married him. Certainly in this day and age she need not have had six children, and if she really wanted that many she must have known she had a lifetime job in bringing them up. She complains that they have no manners but does not attribute this lack to her failure to teach them any. She picks on her third son constantly, although at sixteen he is an exact replica of her when I first knew her. She blames her second son's delinquencies upon a housemaid who is supposed to have corrupted him at an early age, and she blames her employment of a fourth-rate maid upon her husband's low salary, when the truth is that she is dependent upon inadequate service because she treats her maids as if they were the lowest specimens of the genus homo. She clings to the tattered remnants of a musical career that was over before it began, and she does not see that her adolescent ambitions are leading to neglect of her main job in life. The elder of the two little girls has just begun to menstruate at the early age of ten and is already showing a furtive and morbid interest in sex. Mr. L is doggedly doing what he can to develop other interests in his neglected daughter, but he gets little aid from his wife. He is a good man but, like his oldest daughter, a bit colorless and irresolute.

Mrs. L's rather hard life has not taught her much. In the twenty years during which I did not see her she developed the outward signs of middle-age—greying hair, wrinkles, and added poundage—but inwardly she remained the same adolescent who eloped to marry a missionary. Life has not been as rosy as she expected, but instead of growing up enough to bear the disillusionment she has protected herself by projecting the blame for her disappointments upon those about her. At forty her youthful dreams and ambitions have definitely warped her attitude toward life, and I hate to think what she will be at sixty.

Some individuals of education, sophistication, and acquaintance with psychological literature show a curious variation in the general pattern of projection. They say quite frankly that this or that is their own fault, and they point out meticulously that no one else could have been to blame. In spite of their verbalism, however, they continue to act in an immature and irresponsible manner.

ESCAPE BY PROJECTION

Two or three years ago I had a student of this type. During an entire semester she never passed in an assignment on time, but she never gave me any excuse. Each time she said the lateness was her own fault and due to her own carelessness. Such candor was pleasant after many years of listening to a wide assortment of real or manufactured excuses, but it did not result in the slightest improvement or modification of her behavior. Each successive paper arrived just as late as all its predecessors, and in numerous other ways the student proved to be thoroughly infantile. In short, she had developed a sophisticated form of projection. She made of herself a verbal scapegoat, and then promptly turned the goat out to pasture and forgot about it. The whole performance was just words and words, presumably designed to fool the college professor for whom words are a stock in trade.

Whenever people have been exposed to Freudian lingo, the observer must be careful to note the behavior and should not let himself be led astray by beguiling verbalism. If a person who has gone through the motions of accepting responsibility continues to be as irresponsible as before, he is merely using a more refined form of projection. By their deeds ye shall know them!

CHAPTER 12

Escape by Sophistication

I AM aware that sophistication is often regarded as smart, clever, modish, and the ultimate sign of a maturity that sees through life's little dodges to the real reasons behind them. Many a simple genuine soul has twisted himself or herself into a pretzel in an effort to become a sophisticate. The bright chatter, the smartaleck rejoinders, the clichés, the facile wisecracks, and the dubious wit all have to be acquired at considerable pains by most of the people who possess them. The really sad thing about sophistication is that its achievement is an empty victory, because it is only one more escape from reality and maturity and an almost permanent defense against both. The end is either boredom or indulgence in perversions to avoid boredom. Sophistication may put a kick into life for a while, but eventually it takes the kick out and leaves one's days hollow and unexciting.

The sophisticate's life sometimes centers around having cocktails at the right bar, eating at the right restaurant, dancing at the right nightclub, having beauty treatments at the right parlor, making purchases at the right stores, receiving invitations to

ESCAPE BY SOPHISTICATION

the right homes, and attending the right functions. Through all these activities runs the thread of talk, gossip, innuendo, wisecrack, and story. The clever raconteur is greatly in demand, and his listeners rarely ask if the incidents he tells are true. The vaunted wisdom of sophistication seems to an innocent bystander to consist chiefly in disbelieving decent human motives and of assigning to other people's behavior whatever motives seem at the moment to be most titillatingly scandalous. It is not difficult, however, to mislead the wise sophisticate; one merely tells him the truth, which he will not credit, partly because it is too simple and partly because he knows no one tells the truth. The most typical sophisticates I have known have struck me as being under great tension, as if they were straining every nerve to make an impression. So far as I could tell, their ambition was to be gay, bright, casual, a bit bizarre, and amusing—always amusing. If one's barbs of wit were painful to others, that was simply their bad luck.

Reality as it is grasped by ninety-nine per cent of the world is not at all the reality of the sophisticate. This highly refined escapist leaves reality behind him and flees into an artificial world in which the emphasis is upon those things that count for little to the bulk of mankind. It is a brittle and fragile life that can thrive only in the steamheated hothouse of a large city, where wealth and material comfort favor the development of an artificial and superficial existence which would shatter at the first cold breath of reality. There is little that is normal in the hectic gaiety of the nightclub or the scurrilous gossip of the bar.

Like other forms of escape, sophistication allows the escapist to remain childish and irresponsible. There is much lip service to maturity but little action that suggests a personality more advanced emotionally and socially than that of a spoiled adolescent. There is often to be sure an adult mentality at work, but it is motivated and controlled by childish emotional drives. To some, the man-about-town and the career girl who lives her own life are the symbols of mature freedom. To the psychologist they are persons still in their early adolescence who have successfully become interested in members of the opposite sex but have never emerged from the experimental stage that characterizes boys from fifteen to seventeen and girls from thirteen to fifteen years of age. The next stage, that of adulthood, consists in a narrowing of interest to one mate and the end of experimentation. Those who still play the field have never passed out of their early adolescence. The sophisticate's emphasis upon externals is another trait that is adolescent in character. The child puts little value upon externals because he hardly notices them, and the true adult is equally indifferent because he is aware of their unimportance, but the adolescent is tremendously concerned about them. It is almost a matter of life and death for the adolescent to dress as his friends do, talk as they do, act as they do, go where they go, and believe what they believe. This abject aping is nor-

ESCAPE BY SOPHISTICATION 123

mally outgrown, but the sophisticate retains it. He preserves also the intolerance of adolescence toward those who are different from himself or outside his immediate circle of acquaintances. Thus to the psychologist sophistication is a prolongation of adolescence that forms an escape from the reality of adulthood for those timid souls who lack the courage to grow up and prefer to remain dependent upon a small clique for their standards, their ideas, and their interpretations of life.

Romaine Rogers is now a woman of fifty-nine, a spinster, and a private secretary. In her work she is excellent. For many years she has lived in New York City, not because she can earn more there than at home, but because of what she calls the stimulation. When I first knew her she was a pleasant, not too intelligent, industrious, simple young girl in a small town. She came from a distinctly bourgeois background, to which she was by nature well adapted until in her early twenties she became ashamed of it. A somewhat delayed adolescent revolt eventually landed her in New York and in a group of city-bred young people, whose manners, ideas, and clothes she promptly aped with great fidelity. She went to clever shows and learned the lingo of the critic; she went to art galleries and learned the appropriate chatter; she took courses in writing and discovered sonnets; she went to the opera and picked up a smattering of musical shoptalk; she read the latest books—also the reviews of them—and learned to say the proper things. She did not understand any of the material very well, but she got a great thrill out of it. In the course of years she has become excited over a number of different groups—theosophists, healers, mystics, star-gazers, spiritualists, and numerologists. She has never been quite carried away by her enthusiasms, however, because her basic bourgeois horse-sense eventually asserts itself. She has tried her hand at sculpturing, short-story writing, poetry, and piano playing, but without success. She works hard enough, but the spark is not there. If Romaine were happy these numerous gropings might be justified, but she is not. Her life has become one continuous search for a thrill. Her measuring stick for people and experiences is the amount of stimulation she gets from them. She does not see at all that she was never intended to be living the life she leads, nor does she realize that her need for external stimulation comes from a barrenness within herself. She is an average, ordinary, middle-class woman of no originality, who has nothing to say through the media of sculpture, poetry, or music. She has plastered over her native commonplaceness and simplicity with a veneer of attitudes, vocabularies, and habits borrowed from others. In fact she has almost destroyed her original self without having developed another to put in its place. The result is an emptiness of mind and spirit that she tries to fill by syphoning off the stimulating ideas of others. It is improbable that she will ever learn to face her own mediocrity. She has built up too many different kinds of lingo behind which she can retreat. She will probably live out her days in New York, running from thrill to thrill, seeking someone or something upon which she can lean, never happy because she has so few resources within herself, and continually trying to accomplish the impossible feat of warming her emptiness at another person's fire. If she had remained at Dogtown Corners she might have developed into a real person instead of a synthetic one, and she would almost certainly have been happier.

The sophisticate's answer to my classification of him as immature is going to be that I am jealous because I have not the necessary ready wit to be as clever as he is. Probably he would be right. I fit badly into an urban environment where people seem to spend their lives pursuing things that give them little satisfaction when caught. However I have yet to see my first happy sophisticate, and until I do I shall continue to regard sophistication as a complicated but childish escape from reality.

CHAPTER 13

Escape by Illness

THE PERSON who becomes sick whenever the going gets tough is too common a phenomenon to need much description. I suppose everyone has at one time or another exaggerated a slight discomfort into something more serious in order to avoid doing something he or she did not care to do. The permanent escape into illness is the same mechanism raised to the nth degree.

Usually the escapist is running away from a difficult situation although sometimes the illness is a mere bid for attention. A mature person does not fake illness to get attention, and he prefers solving problems to putting his head in the sand and playing dead. Descriptions of people who try to escape life by being sick usually stress the central problem to which adjustment has not been made rather than the immaturity of those who cannot adjust. I prefer to stress the infantilism that prevents the facing and solution of problems rather than the situations, because these are no different from the problems faced by thousands of other people who take effective steps toward solving them. The difference lies mainly inside the escapist. For some reason he cannot stand what other people can, and the fundamental reason is that he is too immature.

In a town where I once lived for many years I knew a family composed of a mother, two middle-aged daughters, and a son of about thirty. One daughter taught kindergarten, the other kept house, and the son worked more or less at casual jobs, none of which he kept for long. The mother was a chronic invalid who had taken to her bed when her youngest child was born and had never left it. She walked out on her responsibilities as completely as if she had gone to Kamchatka. A few years later the father of the family died leaving his wife a tiny income from his life insurance. The oldest daughter took her mother's place as well as she could, but she was also a childish person emotionally. Her mental development was quite adequate for her work, but she showed her immaturity in two ways especially: she read constantly the type of silly, sentimental love story that interests adolescent girls and she developed a devoted affection for one man after another, none of whom returned her enthusiasm. The second sister, like the father, was normal, although both died at an unnecessarily early age because the fatigue of supporting an assortment of weaklings had undermined their health. The son was also an escapist. Whenever something annoyed him he got drunk. He was somewhat more mature than his older sister and he could adjust fairly well to the demands of life so long as no crises arose, but he could not face fresh difficulties. In this one family then there were three types of escapism—one into illness, one into fantasy, and one into drink. The mother and eldest daughter both lived to a ripe old age and both retained almost into senescence the appearance of youth. Rarely have I known people upon whom life weighed so lightly. The mother never left her room and rarely got out of bed; she spent her time in reading, crocheting, sewing, or dozing. The daughter prepared the small meals they needed, went daily to the library for more trashy novels, attended free lectures or concerts, and trailed the man with whom she fancied herself in love at the moment. Since these affairs seemed to involve no heartbreak, one can assume that the feeling was quite superficial. Both mother and daughter had made perfect escapes on a childish or adolescent level.

Mrs. Poindexter was once a rather delicate little girl who was constantly being warned by her mother to be careful of this and cautious about that. She was not much fun to play with because she had had all the recklessness removed from her by the time she was six. As I look back I can see that she probably was delicate. She had a mild case of asthma, little appetite, a chronic cold in the head, and a low general vitality. As she grew older she discovered that she could get her own way by becoming sick and scaring her parents. Her agemates caught onto this dodge very soon and used to slap little Mary Jane when she tried to fool them, but her parents could never feel sure that the symptoms were not real. Sometimes they undoubtedly were.

Mary Jane has now been married for several years to one of the most amiable and interesting loafers I know. He isn't in any sense a bad or even mildly naughty individual; he is simply worthless as a means of support. His wife has had a succession of jobs and has managed to keep the household as a going concern. In some ways she is more mature than the average adult, but she has retained her childhood pattern of flight into illness whenever the going gets too tough. She goes along for months, working every day, apparently in average health. Then something goes wrong either with her work or her home situation and she has asthma, bronchitis, or severe indigestion, accompanied by fainting and nausea. Whenever she is out of a job, she is constantly sick with assorted illnesses that miraculously disappear when she starts working again. Three or four times her husband has found work of not too onerous a nature so far away that he could be home only week-ends, but he never has remained long at work because Mary Jane gets so sick he has to come home. The woman undoubtedly does have some real illnesses, but after forty years of observing her, I have ceased to credit the repeated coincidences between sickness and crises in either work or home.

My old friend has admittedly a hard row to hoe, but she does not hoe it as efficiently as she could because of her childish reactions to strain. She is fundamentally a hard worker and would get along well if she did not so often lose jobs because some minor change that she does not like is introduced and she promptly becomes sick and has to resign. Her husband was at first all sympathy for her poor health, but the relation between his wife's emotional disturbances and her illnesses did not long escape him and he has developed a flippant attitude that all her symptoms are faked, either deliberately or unconsciously. Her troubles thus pile up both at home and at work. I don't care to guess what the end will be, but I fear a nervous invalidism in which Mary Jane will seek permanent refuge from the problems of maturity.

Pauline M was a junior in high school. She had always done good work in all subjects. She was a careful student who prepared her assignments well, often handing in extra assignments because she was really interested in her classwork. On three different tests of intelligence she earned I.Q.'s of 114, 107, and 109. During the first three years of elementary school she had been regarded as an unusually promising pupil. In the fourth grade she had her first experience with examinations. Her teacher was considerably surprised when Pauline's examination were well below the average of the class. She did not, however take the matter seriously, since Pauline was so young. The girl's fear of examinations grew during succeeding years in school. Every teacher had the same experience. Pauline did excellent classwork, showed through her recitations that she had mastered the subject matter, but turned in atrociously bad examinations. She was always passed because her teachers felt so sure she really knew the material, even though her examinations were unsatisfactory. One teacher became interested in the situation and, during the month before the end of school, asked Pauline in class every one of the questions that would appear on the final examination. All questions were answered reasonably well, some of them brilliantly. Yet, on Pauline's examination paper not a single answer was passing.

Pauline was always in a pitiable state when she entered the examination room. She was pale, her hands trembled, she perspired, her voice shook, and she was likely to cry on the slightest provocation. Sometimes she seemed unable to write at all and would spend half the period staring in front of her. During her junior year, things became even worse and Pauline became so sick she had to be excused from three or four examinations. The first time this occurred, she was allowed to make up the test by means of an oral quiz after school hours by the teacher. This test was passed easily and well. Since that time Pauline has never taken a written examination, because she is always too sick.

Pauline comes from a good home where she is the youngest of four children. Both parents are college graduates, the oldest brother is a young doctor, the next oldest is in graduate school, while Pauline's sister, a year older, is a junior in college. All three of the older children have made superior records in school and are regarded at home as being distinctly brighter than Pauline. Pauline has been treated as a child by her family; in fact, she is still called "Baby." Special concessions are usually made whenever she thinks she needs them. The mother reports that in her pre-school years Pauline had marked tantrums whenever she was crossed. Later on, she often became nauseated when she was supposed to do something she disliked. Since she has been in high school Pauline has complained of numbness in her right hand and arm whenever she had a composition or report to write and found difficulty in doing it. Between her temper and her illness she has managed almost always to have her own way.

Pauline fears examinations fundamentally because she is in a panic about failing them and being regarded at home as stupid. When she finds herself in the situation she fears, she simply becomes sick. By this technique she dodges altogether the need of facing the dreaded situation at all, and in addition, receives sympathetic attention during her illness—and what is for her a much easier type of examination later on. There will obviously be no improvement in the situation as long as Pauline is allowed to run away from her problems and as long as her family continues to put so much emphasis on high marks in school.

Like any other form of escape, illness not only arises from childish attitudes but also favors their continuance. Moreover, this type of flight from reality is difficult to modify because it is usually based upon some actual illness. One cannot therefore be sure when the symptoms are real and when they are spurious. Two particularly glaring examples of this point occur to me: a young teacher who had an attack of asthma whenever a disciplinary problem arose in his room and a small boy who had an epileptic seizure whenever he did not get his own way. The young man really was an asthmatic and the child really was an epileptic, but the attacks that arose as responses to strain were of emotional origin and spurious. In such cases the true illness furnishes a ready-made pattern that may subsequently be used whenever the individual is called upon to face an unpleasant situation.

Several ways of escape have been briefly described. All of them have two characteristics in common. They permit the escaper to avoid adjustment to the world as it is, and they permit him to continue his immaturity. He may sugarcoat experience, or hold distorted views, or refuse to look at reality, but whatever the type of reaction he avoids the necessity of growing up and taking his rightful place in an adult world.

PART IV

Solutions for the Mature Person

CHAPTER 14

Living with Yourself as You Are

Perhaps the first and basic step toward learning to face reality in a mature fashion is to assay yourself as objectively and unemotionally as possible. There is no escape from living with yourself, and the sooner you learn to do it well the greater is your chance for contentment.

All people have handicaps—physical, mental, social, or emotional—and most people have a number of them. The handicaps are in themselves of almost no importance; what matters is the attitudes they generate. Some people submit to a handicap, others use it to obtain sympathy or to get out of work, some try desperately to keep it covered, some fight against it, while still others develop a corroding self-pity and think Job should shove over on his ash-heap and make room for them. Actually any effort to run away from a handicap is silly because it runs right after you, and the harder you try to cover it up the worse it shows. In the interests of tranquillity, efficiency, and maturity it is therefore better to look it in the eye and tell it to stop pushing you around.

Physical handicaps are the easiest to see and probably the easiest to adjust to. Various acquaintances of mine are splendid examples of good adjustment under difficult circumstances. Two hunchbacks, a woman with no arms, a blind man, two diabetics, and a cripple come to mind at once. All of them are living normal, happy, mature lives. One hunchback is a popular teacher in a girls' boarding school; the other is married and has three charming, handsome children who are devoted to her. The armless woman is married to a gentle, loving husband and has two normal children. The blind man is a university professor. One diabetic is a newspaper reporter, the other is a lawyer, and the cripple is a superintendent of schools. So far as I can see all of them have normal personalities and mature habits of thought and feeling. People with such severe handicaps are often more sensible about adjusting to them than those whose defects are slighter.

Naturally the person about whose methods of living with herself I know most is myself, so perhaps I may be pardoned if I introduce a bit of personal evidence on this point. For years I was one of the many thousand people who thought a defect would disappear if one just ignored it. I happen to be nervous, excitable, and easily stimulated by the presence of other people. I love humanity in practically all its manifestations, but it certainly disagrees with me. I earned my living by either teaching or doing clinical work—both occupations that keep one among people—but eventually I had to stop because the stimulation kept me so keyed up that by night I could neither sleep nor eat, nor could I devise a way of working without sleeping. Twenty years of frayed nerves, fatigue, and insomnia finally convinced me that I was not intended to live in the bosom of the human family. During the past decade I have finally learned to cut the pattern of my days to the available cloth of my vitality.

LIVING WITH YOURSELF AS YOU ARE

Mental handicaps are harder to see than physical, but the earnest seeker can find his own if he will really look for them. Some people do not seem to have looked. The question is not usually one of general mental capacity but of specific shortcomings of an intellectual nature in people who are perfectly normal or even superior in their mental development. Thus a sincere, competent research worker may lack the trait ordinarily called imagination, while another lacks either the ability or the urge to synthesize his results, and a third has no sense for the practical applications of his work. Conversely the intellectual talents that people have are also likely to be specific. One person's chief usefulness may lie in his ability to devise methods and apparatus for testing theories, while another has a flair for diagnosis, and a third is most successful in interpreting the results of technical experiments in terms that the general public can understand. Part of one's appraisal of himself should certainly be a consideration of his intellectual talents and defects.

One lifelong friend of mine, who is in general a most delightful person, seems quite unable to accept himself as he is. Bill is by nature a warmhearted, sensitive, lovable individual with a lively interest in his fellow-man and the capacity to make himself popular with a wide assortment of people. In addition he has an unusual degree of organizing ability. He can go into an office in which things are tied up in a snarl and have them running smoothly in a short time. Even in his childhood he showed this same talent: he initiated activities, smoothed over difficulties among the participants, and held the group together during a joint undertaking. He belongs to several clubs and is an active member in them, usually being the person chosen to act as chairman of any committee in which friction is likely to occur or through which needed work should be done quickly and efficiently. One would think he might be content with such an assortment of talents, but no, he must try to be a scholar as well, an occupation for which nature never intended him. In the forty-odd years I have known him I have seen him react wisely and intelligently to many a difficult human situation, but for academic pursuits he has no brains. I doubt that he could more than barely pass advanced college courses. About once a year Bill reads a book, usually selecting one that is quite beyond his comprehension, and then he talks about it for two or three months, boring his friends the while. He is not content to delve into a book now and again for his own enlightenment but feels it necessary to lecture his friends upon the ideas he dredges up. Since he is a largely self-educated person—he left school in the eighth grade—he does not know that many of the ideas he derives from his yearly excursions into higher thought are already familiar to those who deal with books all the time. I have known him to explain the doctrine of evolution, in so far as he understood it, to a gyneticist, to lecture a history professor on the economic interpretation of history, and even to present to a statistician a little homily on the nature of sigma. We are all glad when Bill has read his book and recovered from it. He then reverts to being his charming but unintellectual self. If it has ever occurred to him to assay himself, his analysis has not been especially penetrating.

Everyone has some intellectual shortcomings, for which he is generally not to blame. The fault lies in disregarding them. In some cases one can correct a defect, but in others the safest thing to do is to avoid the situations in which the lack of ability would be too great a handicap.

LIVING WITH YOURSELF AS YOU ARE

Readers who complain that my books are lamentably weak in theories are not telling me anything I do not already know. There is little theory in them because there is little in me. I could, I suppose, paraphrase what someone else had written, but I prefer to admit my shortcoming and leave the theories to others who feel they understand them. I can live with myself more comfortably if I do not whip my mental processes into a froth in an effort to be a philosopher. Other intellectual defects of mine may have eluded me but at least I am aware of this one.

Social handicaps are usually easier to locate than mental ones because one's kind friends are so willing to call them to one's attention. The difficulty comes in admitting them. To be sure, some social handicaps can be overcome by a person who is determined to do so, but even so he must first know what they are.

Some years ago I had a young friend who was as eager and anxious to please as a puppy. Nothing made him happier than to do something for someone. He enjoyed such social gatherings as he was asked to attend and he tried hard to be agreeable to others. Unfortunately, however, he had some serious social defects, of which he appeared at first to be quite unaware. To begin with, he was one of the clumsiest boys I ever knew; he could drop anything, and he could stumble even over things that weren't there. At a tea party he could be trusted to spill the tea and drop the toast. His conversation had a similar effect of being beyond his control. He had two types of reaction; either he monopolized the center of the stage, lecturing guests upon a topic of his own choosing and without respect to their interest, or else he sat in a corner and said nothing. Of conversation as a give-and-take arrangement he seemed ignorant. What was to some people even more annoying was his inability to gauge social distance. He was often too familiar, especially with older people, but at other times he was so distant as to give the impression that he had been deeply offended. He liked people and wanted them to like him, but he simply did not know what note to strike. Finally, in his embarrassment at his own ineptitude, he often assumed a pompous and condescending air that grated on everyone's nerves. If the boy had been a recluse by nature these traits might not have been so objectionable, but he loved to be with people. In a vague way he was aware that he sometimes irritated them but he did not know why. One day he asked me what I thought was wrong and I explained to him the shortcoming I have just enumerated and made a few simple suggestions for improving his social skills. For one thing I asked him to try letting his vis-à-vis choose the topic of conversation and to limit his own contributions to not more than three sentences at once, no matter if he did not exhaust the subject. I said he should also make sure that he did not talk any more than anyone else and that he did not try to use the casual conversation of a social gathering as a means of educating his friends in his particular fields of interest. I advised him, moreover, that when he was in doubt as to the desirable degree of intimacy between himself and another person to err always on the side of too much distance rather than too little. For some months he really tried this prescription and improved considerably. At the same time his coordination got better, largely because he was no longer under so much strain. As time went on he made some suggestions of his own, once he had gotten the idea of evaluating himself. His pleasure in social intercourse, his manners, and his interest in people were obvious from the first, but for various reasons too complicated for presentation here he had never acquired certain basic social skills. Although he has made great progress he still shows a certain native obtuseness about his own effect upon others. This trait probably cannot be eradicated, but an objective evaluation of himself and a few sensible remedial measures have done a good deal to bring him the social ease that he has always craved.

The solutions that people find for living happily with themselves are many and varied. The tests of a good solution are a relief from strain, an increased contentment, and a chance to grow in usefulness, but not at the expense of passing the strain and discontent along to others. Some solutions seem on the surface to be positively bizarre. The important thing is what they look like from the inside to the adjuster, not how they appear from the outside to the observer. One unusual but apparently satisfactory adjustment is described in the following history.

Miss X came from a quite comfortable but not socially prominent home, in which she was an only child. As a child she was an undersized, unattractive girl, whose mental level was slightly below average. During her childhood Miss X played normally enough with children in the neighborhood, although she was never popular and was often forced to take some inferior part in games. Other children picked on her more or less, ran away from her when they were tired of her dullness, and generally snubbed her, but she was willing to put up with such treatment for the sake of company. With the coming of adolescence she developed unusually strong drives for dominance and attention and tried in many ways to impress others. She was the first girl of the neighborhood to wear silk stockings, evening dresses, and white kid gloves. She hung around the street corners to waylay boys. She invited other girls, especially prominent ones, into the drugstore and bought them all the ice cream they could eat for the sheer pleasure of being seen with them. In all ways she tried to find satisfaction for her urges by pushing herself forward among her agemates, but other girls usually rejected her offers and considered her a bore. Between the ages of sixteen and twenty one she entered three different boarding schools but was forced to leave each one in turn, partly because she was too dull to pass the work and partly because she soon stirred up trouble among the other girls. During these episodes of schooling she vacillated between two types of behavior. Sometimes she would sidle up to the most prominent girls in the school and ask them to come to her room or to go some place with her. At other times she would burst into their rooms and cry for an hour because no one liked her and she was miserably unhappy. Her frustration thus often showed directly but was almost as evident during her more usual behavior of soliciting attention in spite of continued snubs.

For some years after leaving the third boarding school she remained at home, in a desultory and generally unsatisfactory manner doing volunteer work of various sorts as a means of obtaining recognition. Committee chairman dreaded having her put in their groups because of her constant importunities and her unsuccessful but obtrusive efforts to dominate the other members. During this time she developed a number of mannerisms that made her even more unpopular than before, and she seemed headed for a serious breakdown as one after another of her advances met with rebuff. Presently she was reduced to attending public lectures and concerts as her only means of contact with people. She would settle herself for the evening with some mere acquaintance and would then buttonhole people for days thereafter to tell them that she had attended the function with such and such a family or person.

When Miss X was about thirty years old her parents died within a few weeks of each other leaving her a modest income. During their last illness Miss X hired a pleasant, quite ordinary, uneducated Negro girl to help her with the housework. This girl stayed on after the parents' deaths and became the first person who had ever given

Miss X the genuine affection and admiration that she had craved all her life. Over this girl Miss X could dominate. The two became good friends and continued to live together, Miss X willingly paying the bills. This strangely assorted pair settled down in great contentment. The girl had never known anyone as kind as Miss X, and the latter had never known anyone so appreciative of her. The Negro girl brought friends of her own race to the house where Miss X made them welcome. Few of these friends had completed grammar school, and Miss X's attendance at fashionable boarding schools seemed to them remarkable. Instead of being an outcast, Miss X found herself suddenly popular. Her native ability was probably greater than that of her new acquaintances and her social position was certainly superior. During the years that have elapsed since this change in her circumstances she has lost her mannerisms and has become a well-adjusted person. She lives modestly, uses her extra funds for helping Negro families, is an adviser for several Negro charities, and is living a happy and useful life. Her drives for domination and attention are now satisfied and her substitute reactions have disappeared. She no longer pesters her former acquaintances. She has an abundant social life and she is a leader. She is also far more mature than those who knew her in her earlier stages ever supposed she could be. By any pragmatic test this woman's adjustment is good because it works; it brings her contentment, relieves her of strain, and permits her to be useful. She has had the good sense to assess herself correctly and to quit a society in which she did not fit. That her solution is one that would not satisfy one person in a million is entirely beside the point.

There is more to facing yourself than just looking in a mirror. A true assessment will give some items in both the credit and debit columns. Once you know what you have to work with you can reform some things and adjust to others until you learn to live with yourself as you are, without camouflage and without self-deceit. When this is achieved you will be on your way to becoming a mature adult and you will have learned to face the hardest reality of all—yourself.

CHAPTER 15

Living with Others as They Are

MOST PEOPLE seem to have a secret yen to make over their friends, acquaintances, and relatives into a model that would suit them better. Sometimes the proposed revisions of personality would be for the best, but this fact does not make them any more likely of success. One of the harder things about accepting reality is the realization that people are what they are and that it is easier to adapt yourself to them than to adapt them to you. Not that children cannot be educated out of many faults, or that adults cannot re-educate themselves. It is, however, a rare adult who can be altered by anyone but himself. For instance, my grandfather got completely rid of his irascible temper, sternly curing himself after he had one day hurled a hammer across the room in exasperation, only to have it connect with his wife's forehead as she entered the room and knock her out for several hours. He never lost his temper again, but the reform came from within; his parents, teachers, friends, and even his wife had been trying in vain to cure him for years. Although self-reformation sometimes occurs when the motive is strong enough, people do not usually alter greatly as they grow older. They are what God and their experiences to date have made them, and there is not much that another person can do about it, once they have reached adult years.

Anyone who can accept mankind as it is has made a great step forward in facing reality as an adult. A truly mature person can resist the temptation to reform others except indirectly through his own example and can concentrate upon reforming himself. What I regard as a mature attitude was expressed by an acquaintance when she said that she did not tinker with her friends' personalities because she liked them the way they were—faults and all—because she thought their traits none of her business, and because a program of reformation would bore her to death. I would add a further and very practical reason: that one is almost sure to lose his friends if he tries to glue on a trait here and lop another off there.

It is inevitable that an intelligent person will see faults in those to whom he or she is most attached. Only a young person who is tremendously in love or a child who is uncritical can regard another person as one hundred per cent perfect. Sane people see the faults in others but they simply do not care. It is my own opinion that if another person's virtues outweigh his faults, one has no business asking for more.

Immature adults may take refuge in the prolongation of childish credulity or adolescent hero-worship. As a little girl a woman may have adored her mother; as an adolescent, one of her teachers;

and as an adult, her husband. In each case she sees perfection in the object of her devotion. Such a woman has not matured emotionally and she is ill prepared for the inevitable discovery that her love will not automatically confer sainthood upon those she adores. Other adults have one attack of hero-worship after another throughout their adolescent years and then fall in love upon the same basis. As a means of education hero-worship is excellent if a worthy hero is chosen, because the worshipper strives to copy his model, but as a fundamental pattern of adult life it is inadequate. Sooner or later the feet of clay come into view, and the more abject the worship, the greater the shock at their appearance. The adult has to learn that even the dearest of loved ones is as full of human frailty as any other individual. As a first reaction to this knowledge, the immature person may become cynical and sardonic because he cannot accept the revelation of reality. This attitude is as childish as either blind devotion or unquestioning hero-worship. It is merely negative instead of positive. No matter how cleverly or with what refinements of sophistication it may be expressed, it is still childish.

Accepting people as they are, loving them, faults and all, refusing to give unasked-for advice, showing a great tolerance of humanity and its foibles, admitting an equal right to exist to those who do not especially appeal to you, and being willing to make such adaptations as you can to the personality of others—these are to my mind the attitudes of grown-up people. Such attitudes do not prevent love.

Quite the contrary! They permit love to be based upon truth instead of upon illusion.

I may perhaps be accused of having a defeatist attitude toward humanity. Unfortunately for the development of a cheery optimism I have read too much history. Individual human beings learn much, but it seems to me that humanity learns practically nothing. It is not defeatism to admit what one believes to be true. Each successive generation starts where the preceding one did, but because of accumulated knowledge and better education it can progress faster and further, even though it does not inevitably do so. The time to modify each generation is during its childhood when much can be done, but once people have reached adulthood they tend in the main to become more and more like themselves. Such as they are, then, so they will remain and as such the rest of the world has to accept them.

I will admit that some people are relatively hard to take, but adjustment to them is possible without nearly as much strain as is involved in failure to adjust to them. It is often possible by making a simple alteration in one's usual conduct to get along easily with a person who presents real difficulties. Such was the case with a woman who taught in the same department with me for many years. Those who would not take her idiosyncrasies into consideration sometimes considered her crazy, but in spite of these peculiarities she seemed to me to be within the range of normality as set by practical standards. She has been successful in her work, popular with

her students, and admired by many loyal friends—
a normal enough pattern of life.

Donna Drake is now a woman in her late fifties who
has been characterized by one marked peculiarity. She is
desperately afraid of being touched. It does not seem to
matter who the person is who touches her. At the instant
of contact she becomes green with nausea, the lines in her
face suddenly become deep creases, she begins to tremble,
and she jerks herself away from whoever has touched her.
Miss Drake makes every effort to control these reactions,
but in spite of her they show more or less. In years gone
by she has been known to slap those who touched her in
case they did not withdraw their hand quickly enough. At
present she contents herself with cutting remarks should
they seem necessary, but in general she has become so
adroit at anticipating the slightest physical contact from
another person that there are few crises. Naturally Miss
Drake has no intimate friends of either sex although most
people definitely like her. As long as one does not touch her
she is as charming a companion and as loyal a friend as
one could wish. Some difficulties of adjustment have, of
course, been pyramided upon her peculiarity because many
people will not take the trouble to understand her. Her
phobia is a logical even though extreme reaction to an
experience of her late childhood, about which she told no
one until a few months ago. When she was twelve she was
the victim of a sexual attack by a degenerate. Instead of
rushing home and telling her mother she suppressed the
story. She promptly buried the episode as deeply as she
could and resolutely forgot it. Her later reactions when
she felt herself touched were a continuance of the hysterical, fighting response that was entirely justifiable when
first made. If she had told her parents about the attack,
her first subsequent symptoms of withdrawal would presumably have been attributed to their real cause, and her
phobia might never have developed. It would certainly have
been understood.

There followed several years during which she refused to go on even minor errands alone and gave other indications of timidity, but her parents did not feel that she was unusual. As time went by and she spurned attention from boys—although she was willing enough to talk and joke with them when other people were around—her parents became a little worried, but attributed her reactions to her determination to have a career as a research chemist. They did not see that this determination was a result, not a cause. It was the aloneness of the research work that appealed to her. In the course of time Miss Drake manifested another oddity; she took extraordinary precautions about her health. This attitude was noted by others, many of whom supposed she had a phobia about disease. Actually she had a phobia about being examined by a doctor because she would have to submit to being touched. As usual she concentrated upon preventing a situation in which she might be forced into overcoming her phobia and therefore tried to avoid the need for calling a doctor.

Adjustment to Miss Drake is not difficult. One merely remains at least two feet away from her. Yet there are a number of supposedly intelligent people in her environment who cannot seem to learn this simple form of restraint. They lay a hand on her arm to call her attention to something, or they insist upon shaking hands with her, or they throw an arm across her shoulders. However they are adequately punished, because they lose the devoted friendship of a very charming and stimulating person, when they could by a slight adaptation have kept it.

Instead of adjusting to their parents, their children, their friends, their employers, or their employees, people often insist upon trying to make others conform to them. I do not mean to imply that any one person should become a human doormat in his efforts to let everyone else have his own way, merely that each person should do his share of the adjusting and that each should stop trying to force impossible conformations from others. When the handwriting is already on the wall it is best to read and heed it, instead of pretending it is not there. In the following two instances people were trying to force an adjustment that, in its nature, was impossible.

Henry was a well-developed boy of eighteen who came from an excellent family. He had attended a progressive elementary school, a country day school, and a first-class preparatory school, but now just when he should be ready for college he was failing. His parents were bitterly disappointed over the poor quality of his schoolwork and greatly disturbed over a recent attitude of rebelliousness and resentfulness toward all authority at home.

Upon examination Henry proved to have average mentality, but not a high enough intelligence to attend college. His ability carried him easily through elementary school and into high school, but in the last two years of preparation for college he was already beyond his depth. All during the previous two years he had kept up with the tail end of his class by much extra effort during the school year and by persistent tutoring during his vacations. He had succeeded, however, in passing only one out of six college entrance examinations.

Unfortunately for Henry both his parents had few interests outside the home and their chief occupation consisted in trying to force their only son into doing better school work. They stood over him at home, kept him in his room Saturday and Sunday evenings, hired tutors to push him, wrote him several times each week when he was in boarding school, and generally hounded him.

Henry himself had already concluded that he was intellectually inferior to most of the other boys and he knew his interests were altogether different from theirs. As he put it, "Books don't say anything to me." His defiant attitude at home was presumably an outward expression of his feelings of frustration at being caught in a situation in which he experienced only misery and from which he saw no escape, since his family traditions required that he attend Harvard where his ancestors for six generations had graduated. The academic preparation for college was an intellectual task of which Henry was incapable and in which, in spite of his best efforts, he was doomed to failure. Henry would willingly bow out of the life academic and take a mechanical course in trade school—work for which he has more than adequate ability—but his parents remain deaf, dumb, and blind. They will not accept the fact that their only son has not and never will have the academic brains or the book learning essential for success in college.

Thus far, Henry has done such adjusting as has been done, but he is getting tired of his role. As he grows older his revolt will become more and more evident and in the end the parents will either adjust or be broken. They cannot bend nature to their personal desires, and Henry will never graduate from Harvard. The handwriting is on the wall but thus far they have ignored it.

Mr. Brown is a highly intelligent man with a deliberate, reflective, critical type of mind. He is a bit rigid and conventional in his thinking and he shows only a moderate amount of originality. In disposition he is inclined to be suspicious and secretive at all times and occasionally acutely jealous. His general emotional tone is serious rather than merry, although he is not actually gloomy. His wife has an alert uncritical mind that is certainly far from profound, but she is both facile and ingenious. Her reaction-time is fast, and the kind of thinking she does at all she does on the dead run. She is the type of person who thinks up a new way to hang curtains while she is scrub-

LIVING WITH OTHERS AS THEY ARE

bing a bathtub, or evolves the perfect discipline for Junior while the dentist is pulling one of her teeth. In disposition she is generous, affectionate, and naive; she gives away time, love, ideas, money, or work to anyone who seems to need them. Her emotional tone is cheerful, but she has a tendency to become excited and she loses her temper easily. Mr. Brown's deliberate carefulness looked to Mrs. Brown like security, and her vivacity seemed to him charming and thrilling. All would be well if each were willing to leave the other alone, but the one trait they share is a conviction that his or her way is the only way. Mr. Brown constantly urges his wife to stop and think, the way he does; she gets annoyed because he is unable to think on his feet as she does. He is sure her quickness is nothing but carelessness, and she regards his deliberation as sheer stupidity. She scoffs at his fear that someone will steal his inspirations, and he froths at the mouth when she light-heartedly gives away a good idea. He regards her casual way of picking up acquaintances as in bad taste, and she thinks his caution and suspicion to be cowardly and undemocratic. He warns her that people will criticize her, and she replies blithely, "O.K., let 'em," and goes on her way. She tries to reform his seriousness, and he tries to dampen her gaiety. Each of them has precisely the qualities the other needs, but instead of valuing their individual differences they criticize, deride, abuse, and quarrel—each trying to re-create the other in his own likeness.

These individuals persisted in efforts to make over another person instead of adjusting themselves to his abilities and interests. In the first story the parents' love and ambition for their son were based on illusion, while in the second, neither husband nor wife would adjust to the other's faults or peculiarities, and each wanted to reform the other.

I might add that the person who learns to like

people just as they are gets a particularly nice reward, because he is no longer irritated, distressed, thwarted, or angered by the foibles and absurdities of humanity. He sees them, notes them, remembers them in case he feels adjustment necessary, and goes on his way without resentment. Such an attitude has to be achieved by a person who works in mental clinics before he can reach his greatest usefulness. Otherwise he spends too much of his time getting upset and devotes too much of his attention to the effect other people are having on him. Nothing about humanity surprises, annoys, or upsets an experienced clinician in so far as he is personally concerned. An adult in any walk of life can achieve a similar detachment if he is sufficiently mature. And he will find a contentment and serenity that is denied to those immature adults who cannot accept people as God made them.

CHAPTER 16

Living in the World as It Is

THE WORLD seems always to be in a parlous state if one can believe the contemporary opinion of each age. Throughout the centuries ever since written records have existed, some proportion of the world's current inhabitants has thought it was coming unstuck and would soon fall to pieces. Listen for example to Jeremiah, who flourished about 600 B.C.

> Hear now, this, O foolish people, and without understanding; which have eyes and see not; which have ears and hear not. (V:21)
> Your iniquities have turned away these things and your sins have withholden good things from you.
> For among my peole are found wicked men: they lay wait, as he that setteth snares; they set a trap to catch men.
> As a cage is full of birds, so are their houses full of deceit; therefore they are become great and waxen rich.
> They are waxen fat, they shine; yea they overpass the deeds of the wicked; they judge not the cause of the fatherless, yet they prosper; and the right of the needy they do not judge. (V:25–28)
> Oh that I had in the wilderness a lodging place; that I might leave my people and go from them; for they be all adulterers, a company of treacherous men.
> And they bend their tongues like their bows for lies: . . . for they proceed from evil to evil, and they know not me, saith the Lord.
> Take ye heed everyone of his neighbor, and trust ye not

in any brother: for every brother will utterly supplant and every neighbor will walk with slander. (IX:2-4)

It would be hard for a modern misanthrope to be much gloomier or to hold a lower view of mankind. Such carping criticism of each age may be taken for granted and discounted.

People who feel badly about the world generally take one of three attitudes towards it. Some crusade, some complain, and some fight back. The crusader cannot resign himself to the world as it is and he thinks he can make it better by tomorrow or by next week at the latest. Young people are likely to be crusaders, which is perhaps just as well since experience will soon knock much of the zeal out of most of them, and if they did not start with an ample supply they would have none at all left. Blind enthusiasm for reform is, however, so definitely an adolescent trait that one may question the maturity of the flaming middle-aged reformer. In any case the crusader does not have too good an adjustment to the world about him, because his premises are false in that he believes marked reforms and conspicuous progress to be possible within a short time. He cannot accept a world that is neither good nor on its way to being good, so he ignores such facts as prove an opposite point of view and clings to his private interpretation of reality.

The chronic complainer cannot accept the world as it is either, but he has no hope of being able to do much about the situation. He criticizes this, weeps over that, and audibly wishes something else were different. He has a conviction that the world is an unjust place in which people do not receive their due reward. The complainer also has a perverted idea of reality which he substitutes for facts.

The belligerent person who fights back at the world may have about the same estimate of it as that held by the crusader or complainer. The difference lies in the nature of the emotional attitudes. The crusader feels sure he can lick the world, the complainer knows it has already licked him, and the fighter is afraid it soon will unless he makes a last-ditch stand to avoid being overwhelmed. He therefore tries to remain on the alert for treachery, to attack first, to cover his fear by aggressiveness. His view of the world also is decidedly warped.

Two points especially should be noted about these three typical human attitudes. First they help people through life even though they are based upon inadequate or erroneous conclusions, because they furnish a settled point of view by which new data can be interpreted. Second the attitudes are emotional, not intellectual, reactions and therefore do not show the detachment that characterizes maturity.

An adult should have learned that while human progress does take place, it is painfully slow, and that the most he can do to promote progress is to add to the total forces of good that tiny drop which represents his importance to mankind. Instead of assuming a permanent attitude that will color all subsequent data, he can try to find out objectively what goes on about him and to understand what he learns. He can balance off the good in humanity against the bad, welcoming the former and refusing to be overwhelmed by the latter. He can accept without hysterics the world as he finds it—imperfect because human beings are imperfect, but often delightful because human beings are also often delightful. If he can keep a mature view he will not find escape into delusions necessary, nor will he be crushed by life's ingratitudes. True maturity gives one courage to look reality in the eye and not be discouraged by an extremely human world.

PART V

Maturity and the War

CHAPTER 17

Mature Attitudes in War and Peace

IN THE present national crisis there is much food for thought in the relation of war to human maturity. The war can be fought by young men, but it cannot be won by them. Victory rests upon the abilities and attitudes of entire adult populations. If our attitudes are sufficiently mature we have a chance to win; if they are childish we shall not win, even though our armed forces may put the enemy to rout. At the moment, then, a mature general public is especially necessary.

Maturity has many opportunities to show itself. Thus, an intellectually mature person can get a good understanding of the psychological bases of war, of the reactions of people to their leaders, of the personalities of the various dictators, of the uses and effects of propaganda, of the attitudes toward war shown by adults and young people, by soldiers and civilians, by high school boys and girls, by war workers and farmers, by natives and aliens. Such understanding lays the necessary foundation for the development of mature emotional and social attitudes. One needs to understand also the effects of war upon the direct participants, upon civilians who live in danger zones, upon relatives of fighting men, upon those with dear friends or relatives among the country's enemies. On the home front also there are many critical problems for the solution of which a mature attitude is essential—for instance rationing, price fixing, or strikes. Everyone has to have some attitude on these matters because everyone is affected by them. Finally there will be need for great maturity in dealing with the post-war reconstruction of the world. The possible topics for discussion are so numerous that I have had to choose only a few to concentrate upon although there will be passing reference to many others. The ones I have selected are the psychological bases for war, the common attitudes of various segments of the population, the reactions on the home front toward the numerous restrictions imposed by the war, and the current beliefs as to proper arrangements in a post-war world.*

It almost goes without saying that war itself is a childish method of settling a difference of opinion, aside from being a singularly inefficient one. As pointed out earlier, small boys and girls strike and scratch each other when they are angry, but adults inhibit such immediate physical reactions and substitute for them some form of verbalism which often leads to a reconciliation. War is a reversion on a

* This chapter has been rewritten four times in an effort to keep it up to date as the manuscript progressed through the routine of publication, but during the six months between the present and the date of the book's appearance some sections will again get behind the times. I regret this situation, but there is nothing I can do about it. Time marches on!

national scale to the childish "I'll knock his teeth out" form of response.

War is a regression not only to childish patterns of behavior but also to childish attitudes. If mankind did not show a lamentable tendency to regress in the face of crises, there would be no war. The fundamental fact seems to be that many human beings are unable to adjust themselves to the complexity of modern life; that is, they are by nature incapable of living in large communities, of using widely the almost unlimited power of modern inventiveness, of being welded into groups with common aims and purposes, of solving difficult problems on an adult level without accompanying emotional explosions, of being tolerant under pressure. Mankind therefore tends to regress in an effort to escape a complexity that it does not and cannot understand. To be sure, modern war is technically as complex as modern peace, but in it there is escape for the spirit in its return to a simpler mode of thought and feeling. If this theory is correct then wars cannot be prevented. It remains to be seen, however, whether or not mankind can adapt itself to the complex life that human intelligence has evolved. It is possible that an intensive education of the emotions would eventually produce a generation of true adults, but for this purpose the schools would have to change considerably from the traditional model. However, the power that lies in education has been well illustrated by Germany, Italy, and Japan, for each nation has succeeded in indoctrinating a generation with a specific set of emotional responses. The fact that they are not from an American point of view desirable reactions should not blind one to the efficiency of education to mold human beings. A world-wide education for peace might even stop these periodic regressions of mankind. I sometimes hear people scoffing at education, perhaps because they happen to have had poor teachers or an inappropriate curriculum, but if enlightenment, education, and training in their widest and best sense cannot effect a change in men's reactions to strain, then it is unlikely that the change can be effected. It seems as if all other possibilities had already been tried, and none of them has prevented wars from recurring. Either humanity educates itself out of fighting or, with a few more decades of technological advance in the fine art of killing, there is an excellent chance that the human animal will eliminate himself in sufficient numbers to permit the survivors of such an Armageddon to live a very simple life indeed.

To be sure war, on whatever emotional level, seems at the moment to be the only possible answer to the brute force confronting civilization. Nor will this fundamental problem of power disappear after the war is over. Thus far mankind has evolved no means for meeting force except by the exertion of more force. Perhaps there is no other way, and in that case an end to wars seems impossible. It may be that the international gangster can be stopped by threats at the very beginning of his career, but that once started he can be opposed only by a force greater than his own. In recommending a world-wide education for peace I do not mean a starry-eyed and impractical education that denies the existence of evil. Bad men and women exist and probably always will. The crux of the problem is the early recognition of evildoers, the re-education of those who can be saved, and the control of the incurables. An education for peace does not necessarily lead to a flabby state of either mind or body; it should produce people who, like the citizens of ancient Rome, preferred the scythe but would and could hammer it into a sword if they needed to. Perhaps what I mean is an education based upon reality but permeated by that spirit of love for and tolerance of one's neighbor that constitutes the core of all great religions. If the world is going to be saved from these recurrent situations for which the application of brute force is the only solution, it will be saved through an upsurge of the human spirit, based upon a realistic appraisal of mankind and guided by a deep sense of what is right.

When an individual is faced by a situation he cannot solve, he becomes demoralized, feels insecure, and is willing to barter his independence for guidance and aid. It is to this attitude of mind that the leader makes his appeal. He announces loudly and often that he can lead the faithful out of bondage and into the promised land. People who are already bewildered become his followers, because by so doing they can escape fear and recapture security. The psychological experience is no different from that of the religious man who gives his life to God.

From that point on the leader does the thinking, and the followers do as they are told. The regression is from existence as an independent and mature individual to a childish level of dependence upon and trust in a father-substitute, or in extreme instances a god-substitute.

The rise of a leader in times of stress is a familiar phenomenon and is probably as old as mankind. It has been carefully studied among primitive peoples. Thus, when the Indians of both North and South America lost their tribal lands to the white man and were pushed farther and farther into the hinterland, messianic cults arose spontaneously as leaders announced that they could and would lead their tribe back to its former position of prestige. The people followed these messiahs across burning desert and pestilential swamp, into battle against overwhelming odds, into even more grinding poverty than that which they had left, because the leader had given them hope and courage and something to believe in. In similar fashion Hitler arose in troubled times as a messiah and was followed by the unhappy, defeated, discouraged Germans because he offered them hope, courage, something to believe in, and a renewal of their self-respect.

Any group of people can be driven into becoming docile followers by enough hunger, anxiety, and hopelessness, although some groups succumb to leadership more easily than others, probably because of cultural tradition. Thus the Swiss are confirmed individualists and can harly sink their Tweedledee and

Tweedledum differences long enough to organize against a common enemy; they are also the people in Europe with the longest experience of democracy. Their traditions reflect a sturdy, individualistic, independent, and unconquerable spirit, that was attested to as long ago as the days before Christ and by no less a person than Julius Caesar. A more difficult group to lead by the nose would be hard to imagine. By contrast the Germans are, and for centuries have been, easily led; Tacitus, who lived in the late first and early second century A.D., remarked upon this trait in his description of the primitive Germanic tribes. In addition to a tradition of submission to leadership the Germans have a long tradition of insecurity. The territory that is now Germany was for many centuries split up into more than three hundred small countries, each the prey of its stronger neighbors or of any large foreign power that cared to invade it. During and after the Reformation the Germans of the North were the arch heretics, and their antagonism to Rome robbed them of the security enjoyed by countries that were predominantly Catholic. The long religious conflicts, which culminated in the Thirty Years' War, depopulated whole sections of Germany and wiped out entire villages, as thoroughly as Lidice was destroyed. Within modern times the most important of the German states have been ruled by benevolent despots. A notable example was Frederick the Great who did much for his people and showed them the attitude of a father toward his children. At roughly the same time the extremely unbenevolent despots of France were grinding down their people until the French blew up under the pressure, precipitated the French Revolution, and began their experiments with democracy. The Germans had no such upheaval and no such experience with self-government. About one hundred fifty years ago a movement began to unite "the Germanies" into "Germany," but for many years these patriotic uprisings were put down by means of executions, exiles, or imprisonment for the participators. Such survivors as there were emigrated to some other country, taking their ideals of democracy with them and leaving behind those who liked to follow a leader or at least had no profound objection to so doing. Germany remained an insecure and loose coalition of several small countries until as late as 1870. This combination of prolonged insecurity, of good government under benevolent despots, of voluntary submission to leadership, and of inadequate experience with democracy has produced a population with an immature outlook, a deep sense of inferiority, a marked fear of losing what it has, and a desperate jealousy of its neighbors. The Germans are, however, a sturdy, healthy, intelligent, dynamic people; if they were anaemic and listless they might quietly submit to domination by those around them, but their vitality pushes them into overcompensation. Like the braggart and bully in private life who try to cover their insecurity and fear by assuming a superiority to their fellows, so the Germans of today are full of pretense. They are not content with being brave, but must be reckless; they are not happy as a superior people but must be the one most superior people; they are not satisfied to point with pride to their substantial accomplishments but must throw out their chests and brag, taking unto themselves credit for all human achievement; they are not happy with mere governmental control of conquered peoples but must torture them. This extreme behavior is psychological camouflage by a nation that is unhappy, insecure, childish, and apprehensive. It is not accident that the totalitarian state has taken deepest root in two European countries with the least experience of democracy and the longest heritage of insecurity—Italy and Germany. Moreover they are new nations as compared to France, England, Austria, Greece, or Russia.

The fundamental precipitators of the present war, the dictators, are extremely immature persons in so far as their attitudes towards the world are concerned. Their minds, though warped by sundry prejudices, are reasonably intact, although they may not remain so. The immaturity shows in their personal traits. In the first place, they think they are so important that the world must revolve around them. This attitude is perfectly normal for a four-year-old child but markedly retarded for an adult. A small boy wants the moon, sees no reason why he could not have it, and raises hell when he doesn't get it— in this respect acting like a balked dictator; a little girl flies into a rage because another child is receiving a small fraction of the attention that she is accustomed to absorb all by herself. Because the world has for a moment stopped revolving around them, both go into hysterics. So does Hitler. All children like to dress up in fancy clothes and parade about, throwing out their chests in a manner suggesting Goering or Mussolini. Each tyrant of whom history has record has shown the same childish trait of certainty that he was the exact center of a universe that would continue indefinitely to revolve about him. No attitude could be further from the mature conviction that one is merely a speck of matter that exists for a second of time. We are important to ourselves and to those who love us, but not to the world. Dictators with infantile attitudes toward life have transformed the world into a howling madhouse through their efforts to twist the universe around themselves, just as a spoiled child disrupts an entire family with his egocentric demands. Both child and dictator crave the spotlight. For the former there is a reasonable prospect that experience and education will produce a change in attitude, but for the latter there is no hope at all. Because mature people know there is none, the tyrant eventually gets a knife in his back.

In addition to being self-centered, the dictator is usually an insecure and vindictive person—insecure because of his early experiences and vindictive because he cannot forgive an indifferent world for its former slights. Hitler is a good example of both traits. He is socially a nobody, he comes from an insignificant family—a great handicap in a well-stratified society—he could rise no higher than a second-rate house-painter, and he could not persuade people to listen to him. By his own confession he learned to hate those who were more successful in any field. He hated the rich, despised the educated, envied the successful, and loathed the aristocrats. His entire régime is colored with his personal obsessions. He cannot allow anyone who threatens his security to live, and he kills even those who are harmless if they happen to belong to a group which has in the past aroused his vindictiveness. Hitler has intelligence in some matters but where his emotions are involved he is childish, uninhibited, and resentful.

One is sometimes disposed to agree with Rousseau that "everything degenerates in the hands of man." If the machinery now being used for the destruction of life and property were devoted to productive and peaceful ends, every man, woman, and child in the world could be well-fed, well-clothed, and well-housed. If the inventiveness that has improved the destructive power of machines during only the past two or three years were applied to the arts of peace, a standard of living such as most people have never known could be evolved in a similarly brief time. Men are able to fly in the stratosphere and to walk on the ocean's floor, but they are singularly incapable of getting along with their neighbors. Instead of using their knowledge of physics and chemistry for the greatest good of the greatest number they have prostituted their skill and inventiveness to the ends of war. At the moment it seems as if the chief outcome of all the technological advance from the days of Attila were the ability to kill more people in less time than he could.

In other fields one sees the same misuse of scientific knowledge. Just as the sciences of physics and chemistry have been turned from their rightful objective of enriching life to the perverted end of destroying it, so have the sciences of psychology and education been used deliberately to reinforce already existing hatreds, to create new ones, and to raise intolerance to a level of insane frenzy. Up until the first World War there was relatively little use of what is now known as psychological warfare, but during that period scientists first tried their skill at deliberately shaping attitudes. Whereas in former wars people were left to develop whatever hatreds or prejudices they liked, in this war their attitudes are in large measure artificially produced, forced into being by a misuse of psychological knowledge. If the attitudes thus engendered were always desirable there would be no objection to such an application of scientific facts, but the human nervous system has no native preference for one reaction over another and will learn whatever it is effectively taught. A morally indefensible attitude is therefore as easy to inculcate as any other. The hatreds in the present war have been in large measure produced deliberately and scientifically. For instance, there has always been in Europe as in this country some prejudice against Jews. Once in a while an incident

MATURE ATTITUDES IN WAR AND PEACE 173

stirred up the populace and there was persecution, and at all times there were a few fanatics who wanted the Jews exterminated. Attitudes in the present generation of Nazis are, however, the result of deliberate indoctrination; intolerance and hatred have been taught from the cradle by the best educational methods. The result of this procedure is a permanent emotional immaturity that will do as much to set Europe back several centuries as the physical destruction of war. Both the Germans and the Japanese pride themselves upon having educated a generation of young people to complete loyalty and obedience. Also to permanent childishness in their dependence upon the state and in their nonthinking acceptance of ready-made attitudes. In so far as is possible with human material, both nations have deliberately created a generation of robots. It is depressing to reflect that by the misuse of psychology and education these nations have trained those who are now young adults not only into habits of automatic response and into an inability to manage themselves, but also into what may prove a permanent incapacity to grow up.

During and since World War I people generally have come to realize the vital importance of attitudes in winning a war. As a result inhabitants of every country are being deluged with propaganda aimed at either strengthening or weakening their morale. Even the army, in which some ranking officers are still inclined to regard psychology as a newfangled and useless trimming, has morale officers whose business is to investigate the causes of favorable and unfavorable reactions and to suggest means by which the former can be developed and the latter avoided. Similar efforts are being made to mold attitudes on the home front. Hence the censoring of some items of news that are either already known to the enemy or would be of no use to him, because they might depress the morale of the average citizen at home. Since attitudes are admitted to be of great importance, it would seem worth while to sample a few that are typical.

The American public has demonstrated toward the war its usual wide range of human reactions toward any important issue. We have pro-German, pro-Italian, and pro-Japanese citizens—people who have more friends and interests in an enemy's country than in their own. We have also fanatics who hate every member of one or more of these nationalities with an unreasoning hatred. Rabid isolationists vie with equally rabid interventionists.

Certain people regard Roosevelt as a hero and others merely as "that man." Some individuals and groups seem concerned only with what they can get out of the war for their own advantage; at the other end of the distribution are those who are voluntarily donating time, money, energy, and life itself to their country's needs. One man approves of strikes in wartime because he believes the laboring man is usually so downtrodden that he should use this golden opportunity to improve his condition, while another thinks strikers should be tried for treason.

Of such divergent opinions is democracy made, and one hopes that Americans will continue to disagree violently with one another, but not to the extreme of refusing to cooperate upon issues vital to their common safety. While most people are cheerfully putting up with the restrictions imposed upon them, one still meets those who complain bitterly. Recently I observed a portly gentleman who could well afford to miss several meals in the act of going through a train trying to get his fellow-voyagers to sign a complaint because the train was six hours late owing to constant and unscheduled stops to load or unload soldiers and the dining-car had run low on food and had used what it had to feed the military while civilians went hungry. I suppose no one really enjoyed going for twelve hours with nothing but peanuts for nourishment and missing connections because of the train's delay, but the fat man got no signatures. Although there are many variations of attitude in the general population, the predominant tone seems to me to be cheerful, rather docile, and fairly sane, but also a bit childish. Certainly the public is influenced too easily and too profoundly by whatever local leadership happens to appear, as witness the inexcusable riots in Los Angeles between hoodlums and sailors and the tragic race riots in Detroit. There are too many people who prefer the childish pattern of running away from stern necessities to the adult pattern of adjusting to them.

However, the American public is somewhat more mature in this war than in the last in the matter of believing propaganda and atrocity stories. For a while after World War I it seemed to me that people had swung to the other extreme, overcompensating perhaps for their former naiveté by believing nothing. Indeed the more advanced so-called intellectuals made a religion of debunking as many ideals as they could. They made it seem that smartness consisted in denying all former beliefs and principles; they made fun of religion, morals, accepted attitudes, and even of ordinary decency. Such nihilism may have been good clean fun for them, but the common people who read their writings swallowed the cynicism whole and at least tried to bury any principles they might already have developed. The facile intellectual can perhaps live out his days in the rarefied atmosphere of sophistication without a code of morals, but ordinary mortals, like thee and me, need such out-of-date appurtenances as a God and a set of ideals. Intellectuals, like other humans, rarely profit by history, or they would know that the business of tearing down society, destroying its beliefs, and substituting half understood nihilism is a dangerous occupation. Just as the eighteenth century French intellectual leaders undermined the common man's trust in Church and King and substituted an ideology of unlimited personal freedom, so their successors between 1920 and 1930 helped to produce a disillusioned general public that trusted nothing, considered its neighbors as more likely venal than not, and had a vast indifference toward the moral and social ills of the world. A typical product of this school of thought once spent an evening trying to convince me that Chamberlain deliberately threw his country to the wolves because he and others of his class had rather betray national honor, which was nothing but a phrase anyway, than to lose their investments in German industries; a labor leader would have behaved differently, he argued, not because he was more moral or more devoted to the myth of national integrity, but because he had no investments to protect. The young man refused even to consider my own simple theory that Chamberlain was sincere, honest, conventional, rigid, narrow-minded, easily scared, opinionated, and deplorably stupid.

During the years since the Great Depression the average citizen seems to have achieved a more stable equilibrium than he had either during the last war or during the subsequent decade. He does not believe everything he reads, and he takes propaganda with several grains of salt. At first he was inclined to pass off atrocity stories as something manufactured in some reporter's imagination, but with the passage of months he has learned fairly well to read selectively and to believe what seems to be well authenticated. Most of us now weigh evidence better than we did twenty-five years ago and steer a middle course between naïve trust and cynical disbelief. We also stay away from movies designed to arouse hatred, because we know that an emotion thus stimulated rests upon a false foundation.

A marked change in attitude since the first world

war may be seen in the lack of opposition to the learning of an enemy's language. I recall one vivid scene in 1917 when the high school pupils of the city where I was then living met in the central square, made a bonfire, threw all their German books on it, and danced around for a couple of hours singing national songs. Enrollment in German classes decreased almost to the vanishing point. In this one respect at least Americans have shown progress in maturity. There is now great demand for anyone who can speak, read, or write the languages of our enemies, or of people in those countries we are likely either to invade or to be allied with. I know one man who is teaching Turkish, another who is compiling a Mongolian dictionary, a third who teaches modern Greek, and a fourth who has classes in Hindustani. Courses in Italian and Japanese are crowded, and those in German are full. Both the army and navy maintain special schools for training in Japanese, since there are relatively few Americans who know the language. No one with linguistic ability or linguistic knowledge is being wasted. This mature attitude on the part of governmental and military leaders has been reflected in the lower schools, and no such wholesale boycotting of German classes has appeared as was the case during and after the last war.

The attitudes of adolescents are especially important because from them will come the soldiers and citizens of tomorrow. Their reactions are of course varied, but a few modes of response are outstanding and common. Perhaps the most frequent, especially at the beginning of the war, was a feeling of bewilderment, frustration, and uncertainty; the youngsters did not see any future for themselves either during or after the war. They would fight, and many of them would die, before they even had a chance to begin the sort of life they had planned. Even assuming that they lived through the war, they wondered what they would return to, whether or not they would be able to go on with their education, what they could do to earn their living, how they could readjust to civil life. The more intellectual young people struggled continually with these problems, while the less thoughtful resolved the conflict by determining to have all the fun and all the experiences they could while life and freedom were still theirs. Some boys were frankly terrified, some were thrilled by the excitement of a brand-new life, and still others began voluntarily the toughening process that they must all undergo as soldiers but without the accompanying discipline, with the result that the juvenile delinquency rate rose sharply.

During the past few months however, since the boys and girls have had time to hear a good deal about army life from older brothers or friends already in the service, their confusion of mind and soul has diminished and a more positive attitude has developed. The youngsters have heard of one case after another in which the army has sought out a young man's talents and interests for intensive training, and they realize that after their basic training they can probably go on with what they want to do anyway, unless they discover something else they prefer. The army's effort to get each man into the work for which he is best fitted and to provide him with whatever training he needs is bearing fruit in the attitudes of those adolescents who are just below draft age. Many are still apprehensive at times, but most of them look forward eagerly to their army years with the feeling that their service will permit a continuation of their interests and will lead directly into their life's work. That is, their years in the army will not constitute a sharp break in their lives, either when they enter or when they leave the service. This new attitude is healthier, saner, and more mature than the earlier defeatism, and is a tribute to the enlightened handling of its manpower shown by the army and navy.

A few typical attitudes of adolescents are illustrated in the following studies:

One of my friends has a son who was eighteen in March 1942. He had time to finish his high school course before being drafted. He was intending to become a lawyer and to enter his father's firm as soon as he finished his education. His average mark for the first two and a half years of high school had been ninety-four per cent; for the last half of his junior year it was ninety per cent; and for the first half of his senior year, eighty-one per cent. These marks reflect the boy's increasing uneasiness and decreasing interest in the program of studies that had fascinated him for nearly three years. The call to his draft board brought the war suddenly home to him, and he was badly upset for several days afterwards. By the middle of his last semester in high school he was failing every subject, whether from preoccupation with other matters or as a subconscious wish to be given another semester of freedom was not clear. Moreover he had developed a hectic social life and was out late almost every night in the week. In consternation his parents hired a retired but experienced and skillful high school teacher to tutor him. She managed to penetrate the hard outer shell that the boy had developed to hide his disappointment that he might never be able to fulfill his youthful ambitions. By the end of the semester he had pulled his work up to a passing grade and, more important, he had learned a resignation toward the necessary interruption of his life, and he had made alternative plans which, while not as satisfactory as the earlier ones, nevertheless gave him security and peace. The incipient wildness that had fortunately not led him into any real trouble disappeared. He was perhaps a little more insistent upon having a good time than he would have been normally, but he was fortunate in having learned to see the war as a postponement of his plans not as a cancellation of them.

Ralph is a young man of twenty-three who has considerable artistic talent. When the war began he was enrolled in art school, happily and indefatigably engaged in learning portrait painting. He is by nature a cheerful lad, a bit Bohemian, very sensitive to beauty, avid for new sensations, intelligent, and a hard worker. He was drafted within two weeks of Pearl Harbor, before he had had time to get used to the idea of going to war. He disliked the routine of army life intensely and found much in his daily work that offended his sensibilities. His adjustment was gradual and is still not more than passable. For some months he was in constant trouble for minor infringements of discipline, but after a while he developed a flippant attitude toward the entire situation and adapted himself by taking everything lightly, amusing himself by drawing clever if somewhat ribald cartoons, and joking constantly. He has become a good mechanic and is assigned to an airplane base as a member of the ground crew. He is still a minor trouble-maker more as a result of his attitude than of his overt behavior which conforms well enough, but his lighthearted wisecracking keeps the men around him from putting their whole attention on their work. Twice he has been transferred to the drafting room by officers who had the idea that he would prefer to work there and might buckle down to business better, but each time he has been so uncooperative and his work has been so bad that he did not stay long. In the opinion of his officers he made errors on purpose, although they could never prove that he did. Ralph regards himself as one of a lost generation, condemned by a perverse world to tinker with engines when he craves a brush and palette. The work in the drafting room had just enough similarities with painting to remind him too vividly of what he is missing. His one desire is to forget his former ambitions, thus relieving himself of emotional strain. To make life bearable he has achieved an escape into flippancy and indifference to his personal fate. He does not expect to survive the war and he is sure that if he does he will be too blunted in his sensibilities to succeed in the only field in which he has real interest. He refers to himself and his comrades as "the dead who won't lie down." His attitude is that of an old man who has been forced to spend his days in uncongenial tasks and now seeks only peace. As long as he can remain numb he can conform outwardly to military life, so he prefers to feel nothing lest he feel too much.

Frederick was only sixteen when the war started and therefore had time to adjust himself to the idea of being a soldier before he had to become one, and time also to learn many things about army life, both its advantages and disadvantages. He asked questions of older men, read descriptive pamphlets gotten out by the services, and watched for stories of individual soldiers in magazines and newspapers. At school his work was so selected as to prepare him for the job of being a soldier. His work in physical education was designed to toughen his body, his academic work to give him basic skills and to develop his understanding, and his vocational work to help him in preparing for his part in the war and for his later activity. His strictly academic courses were only two, mathematics and modern European history. In addition he was required to take a course that was frankly an effort to teach patriotism. The teachers presented such facts as would show the boys and girls that the American way of life, though by no means perfect, had values that could not be found elsewhere, values that were so important to the pupils as individuals that they must be preserved at all costs. This course was not a sentimental, jingoistic appeal but a carefully thought out presentation of facts and ideas, aimed at the formation of desirable attitudes towards the war. The vocational guidance course was designed to give pupils information about vocational opportunities both in and out of the army and to help them plan their activities so as to incorporate their years in the service into their whole lives without any more of a break than necessary. Finally Frederick had to have one pre-trade course on his schedule; to meet this requirement he chose a laboratory in metal working. The high school thus contributed much to Frederick's development along several lines. As the school year progressed he gained physical, mental, and emotional poise. His understanding of the war situation and of his part in it was more mature than that of many an adult. Moreover the vocational courses guided the boy into making a decision about both his future vocation and the special training he might hope to get in the army. He decided to become a maker of precision instruments. His teacher in metal work thought he had the necessary manual skill, the job interested him, the services were clamoring for more skilled labor of this type, and there was a steady demand for it in times of peace. At the beginning of what would have been his junior year, Frederick entered the army. After his three months of basic training he was sent to a school for intensive work in the making of precision instruments. There he remained for six months of highly concentrated work both in actual construction of parts and in additional mathematics. Frederick is now permanently located in an army camp where he spends his days happily assembling new instruments or repairing old. He likes the work and realizes that he has made more progress in one year of army training than he would have done in three years of ordinary civilian effort. He hopes to be sent abroad for repair work nearer to the scene of action than he now is, but even if he remains at home he will not be discontented. In general his two years of high school prepared him well for achieving an integrated life and point of view. To be sure he has missed for the time being at least the cultural courses that he would normally have taken before he started to specialize, and it remains a question whether or not he will ever make them up.

Donald has shown a different type of reaction. From his fifteenth year, when the draft first went into effect, he has been all agog to join the navy. He has read constantly about the navy and has pestered his parents for permission to join at once. He is really needed at home since his father is crippled, his mother in need of an operation, and his sister too young to support the family. The father has a pension, but it is not enough for three people to live on. Donald should stay home and work for six months, giving his mother a chance to have her operation and recuperate and letting his sister get a little older. His draft board would not take him at once even after his eighteenth birthday, because he would have two dependents. As soon as his mother was again well she could go back to work and relieve him. This plan does not appeal to Donald. He thinks, talks, and dreams about the navy. He has twice tried to enlist, once under a false name. Recently he has developed a habit of going into bars frequented by sailors and pestering them with questions. When sent on an errand he may go blocks out of his way to follow a group of sailors and listen to their chatter. His schoolwork is barely passing, and he is often absent without excuse. There seems to be no reaching Donald with arguments or pleas. Indeed he acts as if he were hypnotized. It is probable that his parents will soon sign the necessary papers to let him enlist in the navy, since the boy is of no use to them in his present condition and is likely to do something silly if his desires are balked too long. At the moment both his crippled father and his fifteen-year-old sister are looking for work so that the mother can go into a hospital. Donald, the logical one to stay at home and take the burden, will be sailing the ocean blue and leaving his family to get on as well as it can without him.

Christine is a very young college graduate who has just begun work on her first job. All during her senior year of college she had been engaged to a young man who had graduated a year earlier. The chief bond between them had seemed to be that they had lots of fun together and found each other endlessly amusing. Christine had always been rather hoydenish and as late as her last year in college seemed unformed and unpoised, except during class hours. Her first reaction to the war was that she and Dick would marry at once and seize their happiness while they could. Her parents and her fiancé combined to talk her out of precipitate action however. During the past year Christine has shown the undramatic, quiet, gradually maturing of mind and character that is appearing everywhere among girls of all classes in their late adolescence. She has developed poise, a reasonable maturity, understanding, dignity, restraint, and an unexpected sweetness and patience. The tomboy and hoyden have been replaced by a responsible young women who is busying herself with a useful job while waiting patiently for her fiancé to return from war. During his training period she saw him often, but she does not at present even know where he is. There is nothing dramatic about the changes that the war has produced in Christine. They are typical feminine developments one sees everywhere, the adaptations that prepare women for the resigned waiting that has always been their lot in times of war. Christine's habits of life have not been greatly affected as yet, although they soon will be since she will probably join the WAVES within a few weeks, but her character has broadened, deepened, and sweetened. She has developed new interests in Red Cross work, in homemaking, in cooking, in child care, in diet, in health. Under normal circumstances Christine would not have reached her present level of maturity before she was thirty-five, if then, and it is doubtful if her innate fineness would have come to the surface except under pressure. She illustrates well the typical effects of war upon the youthful feminine mind and disposition—effects that are quiet and commonplace but which put a girl through a period of emotional toughening analogous to that of the young soldier, as a preparation for her rôle in wartime.

Myrtle, aged sixteen, is typical of many adolescent girls all over the country. In the early days of the war she was merely excited and restless but did not make any move to alter her habits; as soon as uniforms began to appear in numbers upon the streets, however, she went simply hysterical about them. She fell in love with one soldier or sailor after another, stayed out late at night, left school altogether, walked the streets looking for chance pick-ups, and forsook her former friends. Her parents tried to restrain her, but when they began to put real pressure on her, she simply left home and lived in hotel rooms with one man after another—one of the feminine army of camp followers that always trails in the wake of armed forces. One man finally attracted her more than most and she followed him about the country for several months, not however ceasing to be with other soldiers more or less. Eventually she was picked up by the police as a vagrant and sent to a detention home. Contrary to appearances, Myrtle is not a bad girl. She has little interest in sexual experiences, and she is not vicious. In ordinary circumstances she would have had a series of harmless puppy-love affairs under the supervision of home and school. The war happened to coincide with the silly, sentimental, romantic stage that most female adolescents pass through, and she went uniform crazy instead of working off her emotions by reading sentimental love stories and gazing longingly at local football heroes. Because of unsettled conditions she was able to wander about for a long time before the police caught up with her. By the time Myrtle reached the detention home the fever had pretty well burned itself out, and she was no longer thrilled into ecstasies at the sight of a uniform. After treatment for the venereal disease she had contracted, Myrtle willingly went back home and returned to her class in high school. She escaped from this form of war hysteria more lightly than many girls because she did not like the life into which it led her and was glad to get out of it. In less extreme forms this low resistance to a uniform seizes most adolescent girls sooner or later, as parents and teacher very well know. It is one of war's inevitable emotional hazards.

Two of my acquaintances, a brother and sister, have impressed me as having what might be regarded as the typical reactions of youth to war. Bert began by being furiously angry at the Japanese and by joining with several of his classmates in a general boycott against Japanese students in his college. This phase lasted less than a week and was followed by a longer period during which the personal implications of the war began to sink in leaving Bert dazed and confused. The third phase, which began perhaps six weeks after the start of the war, was one of resentment against the whole world because the war was going to upset his plans. The worst of the resentment soon died out, but he remained restless and confused, both intellectually and emotionally. Bert didn't know from day to day what he thought, and his mood varied from gloomy foreboding to outbursts of patriotic enthusiasm. His college work suffered somewhat although he continued to do a moderate amount of studying and to get passing marks.

One of his problems was whether or not to get married before he was drafted. Twice he and his girl set out to elope but changed their minds en route. In the end they decided to wait. After many fluctuations of attitude and mood about the war, Bert has finally settled down to the point of view that it is a necessary nuisance, but that he must do his small share in bringing the world back to normalcy. He is now in the army, he works hard, he has earned two promotions—and he detests the whole business from the bottom of his soul. He still gets annoyed when he thinks of the postponement of his college degree, of his subsequent professional training, and of his marriage by God knows how many years, but he does not let this attitude interfere with his work. He is convinced that the harder everyone pitches in now, the sooner a dirty job will be over. Conspicuously absent from his reaction is any notion that war is glorious or even exciting. He knows it to be cruel, exhausting, and horrible. The more he learns of it the more deeply he hates it and the more anxious he is to get it over quickly. The most interesting thing about Bert's reaction is his rapid maturing under pressure. His anger against particular Japanese has become a hatred of war, cruelty, and injustice; his personal ambitions have become submerged in the stress of group needs; his early confusion and bewilderment have vanished in the face of better understanding. In short, a year ago Bert was an unformed, undisciplined boy, whereas now he is a self-controlled man, with an adult body, an adult mind, and an adult pattern of emotional response.

At the beginning of the war Bert's sister Irene was more stable and mature in outlook, although a year younger. She was also more docile in accepting things as they are, perhaps because she had not yet formulated plans for her own life as clearly as her brother had done and could therefore turn more easily in whatever direction circumstances forced her. Moreover she had no romantic attachments to complicate matters. For a few weeks after the war began she went on her way as usual, taking an intelligent interest in developments but not supposing that her life was going to be directly affected. Slowly it dawned upon her that this was everyone's war. She then wanted to drop out of junior college at once and go to work in the shipyards but was persuaded to finish her freshman year by a promise that she should be allowed to work during the summer. For the first month of the summer she drove a Red Cross truck during the morning and spent the afternoons learning to weld. Then she held a job in a shipyard until school opened in the fall. She did not especially want to return to school, but when she found that by transferring some credits from two previous summers and taking a heavy schedule she could graduate in one more semester, she decided she had better reach a normal stopping point in her academic career, in the interests of her life after the war if for no other reason. During the semester she was rather restless and complained that she was doing nothing useful, but she did graduate in February of 1943. For some weeks before her graduation she had seriously considered joining the WACS but was not altogether sure that such service was the thing she could do best. While she was making up her mind she took a temporary job in a munitions plant where she was assigned to a minor job at the plant's proving grounds. Here she discovered just what she could do that would satisfy her desire to participate as directly as possible in the war and to use the particular talents she possessed. Somewhat to her surprise she found that she was a dead shot, although she had never even thought of shooting off a gun before. At once she determined to find her proper niche by testing guns. She set off as soon as possible to the Maryland proving grounds where she is still employed happily, usefully, and for the duration. Irene has had no such revulsion of feelings as her brother, and she has never been as emotionally involved in the war as he. She has taken the war as it came, adjusting herself as best she could, and finding more excitement than strain in her work. It is likely that she will emerge from the war without serious emotional scars and

and will look back upon it as an interesting experience. Irene is not callous to the world's suffering, but she has evidently decided that there is nothing she can do about it beyond testing guns, investing in bonds, and practicing first aid one night each week. Although she has done as much as one could expect from a young girl, she has not yet suffered except perhaps a little vicariously while reading the newspaper. The war has redirected her energies and reshaped her life, but it has not affected her emotions deeply, nor has it stirred her imagination. Her history of trial and error is common among girls and young women although many others have more emotional reaction than she has thus far shown.

The attitudes described and many others are to be found among adolescents upon whom the war has placed burdens that some of them are ill prepared to bear. Because they have physical strength and stamina one is likely to forget that their immature viewpoints make them more subject than older people to stress and strain and less capable of seeing a situation in an objective light. Some of them mature rapidly under pressure, but many others find adjustment in a cheerful and childish docility; they do as they are told without questioning the basic principles involved and without trying to understand more than their own small tasks.

Regression to childish modes of behavior has in the past been inherent in the demands made upon the common soldier by the life military. The professional soldier gave over his life to his officers, even unto minutiae; he lived by routine and did as he was ordered. Young civilians who at the present time enter the army soon learn the trick of relaxing and letting their officers do much of their thinking for them. From a psychological standpoint they thus become children again. If they remain in the army long enough they may lose the rugged independence of the average American young man. Since civilized people have the greatest difficulty in either bearing or watching pain the soldier regresses in self-defense to the unemotional brutality of childhood. And because some things that a soldier has to do seem to him pointless while others seem heartless, he develops a hatred for his enemy that will carry him through weeks and months of monotony and will bring him in mental safety through the nauseating business of murdering other human beings. These changes are necessary and inevitable under war conditions. Failure to obey lands one in the guardhouse, and the madhouse yawns for those who cannot be emotionally toughened. A soldier has to be a grown man in physical strength, courage, endurance, and intellect, but emotionally he is forced back into childhood.

It is true that at present the average soldier is encouraged to have more independence than was formerly the case. In the main outlines of their attack they follow orders, but they have to fill in the details as they go along, according to ever shifting circumstances. They are therefore not nearly as dependent upon authority as they have been in former wars, and they are trained to some independence of thought and feeling. The blind obedience that produced the charge of the Light Brigade is no longer admired; as a French general watching it said, "It's magnificent, but it isn't war." There is probably less regression among soldiers than there used to be, but there is still some and in individual cases there may be a great deal. Any communal life fosters some types of immaturity, and the army is no exception.

A proportion of our nice American boys will return from the war hardened and brutalized. The main reason that Japanese and German soldiers are more brutal than ours at the moment is that they have been fighting longer. Moreover they lack the mellowing influences of Christianity, the Japanese because they prefer their native religions and the Germans because they have been brought up in contempt of all religion. When one considers the power of Christianity to stimulate men into the do-unto-your-neighbor-as-you-would-have-him-do-unto-you attitude, one can see why dictators want none of it. A soldier cannot afford to abide by its creed and love his fellow man, for if he did he could not fight. Whatever one may think of the mystical or the theological elements in various religious sects, it should be clear that Christianity—if taken literally—could sabotage a nation's war effort.

Against the possible regression of army life at least three positive factors are to be balanced: the educational advantages, the broadening effects of travelling about in a variety of places and of meeting a variety of people, and the self-discipline that is inherent in any military undertaking. Many a boy who in civilized life would have pottered about for years and perhaps never have found a satisfactory vocation is being educated by the army or navy to do useful work that will furnish him with a vocation in subsequent years. Whereas he entered the service with nothing of economic value but his youth and strength, he will leave it with a set of skills that he can sell to future employers. The same thing holds true for girls in the services. Incidentally, the educational programs of army and navy are having a retroactive effect upon the public schools, especially the high schools, with the result that students are getting more and better teaching in mathematics, languages, and science than they ever had before. In addition to the direct education given boys or girls who can profit by it, there is the indirect education of communal living and wide travel. Life in barracks has the same appeal to the young of both sexes that life in college dormitories has always had. The great majority of young people have, however, never lived in dormitories, and their army experience is their first taste of close communal living with members of their own sex and age—and most draftees are still young enough to enjoy it. Moreover many boys and girls who would under normal circumstances rarely leave their home town are being sent where they see places and people that they would otherwise never have seen. The disrupting effect of being taken from familiar surroundings is thus offset by the broadening influences provided for any young man or woman who has the intelligence and desire to take advantage of them. Many a man now in his middle age was taken from his small home town by the draft during the last war, transplanted for a year to foreign soil, and returned to civilian life with a brand new set of interests and enthusiasms that he could hardly have developed if the even tenor of his ways had not been interrupted; and besides, he had had the time of his life. Finally there is the discipline of the army or navy, at first imposed from without but eventually self-generated. Parents and school teachers labor more or less successfully with this problem all the time, but the former are handicapped by affection and the latter by inadequate authority. Moreover, there is in civilian life always a group of people who believe that freedom consists in a perpetual revolt against constituted authority and orderly routine of any type, and from such adults a proportion of each rising generation takes its cue. Unfortunately the schools are poorly equipped to deal with the bright smart-aleck who willingly accepts such minor punishments as come his way in return for the open admiration of his agemates. Once in the army, however, his customary pattern of behavior meets with little or no approval from his comrades and calls down most unpleasant penalties upon his head. The army had much rather a recruit would adjust himself to the demands of his new life and acquire the virtues of obedience and responsibility as quickly and painlessly as possible; but if the young man refuses to bend, the army has the impersonality and the authority to break him. Gradually the external control merges into self-control, and in a few months the army usually manages to finish the education for self-discipline begun by mothers and nurses the day a child is born.

The values of army life thus to some extent offset the faults. The balance could be made even better if the army would muster men out of service, not mechanically, but after a period of readjustment. Just as there is a period of preparation for war, so there should be one of preparation for peace—a period during which every effort should be made to untoughen the boys, especially those who had been at the front. Since the human animal is highly modifiable, a sufficient amount of rest, supervised relaxation, and re-conditioning of emotional response should result in a lessened carry-over into civilian life of those attitudes that are essential to war but destructive of peace. Demobilization of each soldier would therefore depend upon the extent to which he had recovered his civilian outlook, plus the opportunities for work in his particular field. Under such circumstances the re-absorption of several million soldiers would be easier than heretofore although it would take more time, since each man would be discharged only when he was ready, just as he was sent to the front only when he was ready.

Speaking in general terms, the soldier who is subject to shell shock is the man who for some reason cannot be toughened and brutalized, even temporarily. He persists in thinking and imagining, instead of simply obeying. He is usually no more fearful of his personal safety than other men, but he is too high-strung, too civilized, too sensitive, too full of inner conflict to devote himself with single-hearted vigor to the often revolting and always nerve-straining work he is supposed to do.

I know one young bombardier who is an excellent shot and should be a useful combat officer, but he has to be kept at home teaching other young men to be bombardiers. As long as he was dropping bombs for practice upon inanimate objects his work was outstandingly good, but he goes to pieces when he knows there are human beings where his bombs will fall. On his first bombing raid he did not drop any bombs at all, because his imagination conjured up such a vivid picture of the results that his trigger finger froze. He was given a second chance on the principle that he had merely had stagefright, but again he was unable to do anything. He returned to his base in a state bordering on hysteria quite convinced that he was a coward and had disgraced himself forever. In former wars he would probably have been severely disciplined for neglect of duty, but the army has been showing remarkable intelligence in its efforts to understand its men and to get each into the place where he will be most useful. Instead of punishing him for what he could not help, the army sent this young man back to America and assigned him to teaching. In response to this treatment he has developed into a superb teacher and is pulling his weight; moreover he has lost the feeling of shame that he once had. This lad's war experience was short and he was well handled. Had he been forced into fighting or had his spirit been broken by either a retributive justice or ridicule, he might now be in a hospital with shellshock. He has a marked inability to adjust himself to the fundamental conditions of war. This boy is actually no coward—plenty of satisfactory bombardiers would quail at the prospect of going up in the air with a green recruit who was just mastering the rudiments of flying—but he is oversensitive. He would doubtless defend himself if an enemy rushed at him with a bayonet, but he cannot learn to kill in cold blood, a trait that makes him a bad soldier but a good citizen.

The attitudes of the adult general public, the adolescents, and the fighting men, taken together, make up the morale of the nation. Because morale is so important, every effort is being made to build it up and to keep it at a high level. Wars are won not only by tanks and guns but by the spirit of all the people in a nation.

Maturity of outlook has plenty of chance to show itself on the home front. One may well start with a discussion of the reactions to food scarcities and rationing. The government evidently assumed in the beginning that Americans were reasonably mature; officials therefore announced sugar and coffee rationing in advance. The reactions were positively infantile. Thousands of uninhibited adults stormed the stores and laid in such large supplies that a really acute shortage resulted. Learning something but not enough from this experience, the government announced the rationing of canned goods in advance, but accompanied it by widespread appeals to patriotism. The next day the sale of canned good rocketed as unpatriotic but also immature citizens assured themselves of adequate supplies. Realizing finally that it had to deal with a childish general public, the government simply announced the shoe rationing as of right now. A day or two later canned meat, not previously affected, was rationed without warning, because housewives had been rapidly cleaning the shelves during the week when other canned goods had been frozen. The American people despite pleas of all kinds would have produced more serious shortages than now exist if the butchers and grocers had not intelligently, though without authority, put limits upon the amount they would sell to a single customer. They even found it necessary to remember who had already visited their store each day, so as to prevent the same person from getting six times his share by coming to the store six times a day. The reactions of the buying public have indicated not only immaturity but the beginnings of primitive panic. Once rationing started, as with sugar for example, the panic died out, because a paternal government had eliminated the problem of individual choice in the matter. The whole thing has had a reminiscently childish ring. If three children are fighting over the cookie jar and Mother intervenes, seizing the jar and dealing out two cookies to each young combatant, there is almost instant peace; to maintain it, Mother puts the jar on the top shelf, tells the children to find out from her just how many cookies they may have each time they want some, and threatens them with dire results if they try to sneak one out of the jar when she is not looking. The government has resorted to precisely this familiar educational pattern. If all adults were automatically mature, ration books would be unnecessary because people would ration themselves.

The most startling example of panic buying that I have happened to witness lasted hardly twenty-four hours but was of high intensity. The rumor that soap was to be rationed started from nowhere early one morning. Telephones jangled as housewives relayed the news to each other. By eleven o'clock there were queues of people waiting to buy soap. Grocers and drugstore clerks were taken completely by surprise. At first they thought the raid ought to mean something but presently, after calling various jobbers and finding that there was no shortage, they began trying to reassure people and to persuade them to stop buying. By noon they had set an arbitrary limit of two cakes of soap and one box of powder for each sale. Nevertheless, all soap was gone from the shelves before evening. There was no shortage and had been none, nor did any develop subsequently. This one day of panic buying would have precipitated a temporary local shortage, however, if the grocers and druggists had not kept hidden the unopened cartons they had in their stockrooms and pretended to be sold out.

One characteristic of maturity is the ability to sacrifice present interests for the sake of future values. Adults who insisted upon taking a long automobile trip just before gas rationing started were immature as well as irresponsible. They were not willing to give up the small pleasure involved in one last fling, and they seemed to think that because they had circumvented a restriction they had circumvented the results of their own foolishness—but they will be the first to complain when their tires wear out. In the West where there was no gas shortage, rationing was nevertheless necessary to make people stop burning up the rubber that they had been told repeatedly could not be replaced. The entire rationing program is mute evidence of an apparently permanent childishness at least in the American public and perhaps in all humanity. Even now, after two years of war, one frequently sees articles in newspapers and magazines, still explaining patiently to the general public that tires for pleasure cars cannot be replaced for a long time yet and that care of the old tires must be continued.

I happen to live in a part of the country that has become jammed to overflowing with defense workers. One can find among them all kinds of people, from sixty-five-year-old grandmothers to fifteen-year-old high school freshmen, from college professors to illiterates, men and women of fifty nationalities and a thousand peacetime pursuits. On some shifts and in some plants women predominate, the big ones running cranes and the little ones crawling into small spaces to attach wiring. Probably the first reactions of the new war worker are to the noise, the pressure, the confusion, the crowded housing, and the fantastically high wages. Before long he discovers that the cost of living, in spite of price restrictions, is also high. On the whole, however, he makes appreciably more than he spends, perhaps for the first time in his life. One would expect the average laboring man to be happy, especially after he has gotten himself and his family settled comfortably, but he is not satisfied. He wants even more pay and shorter hours; he objects to the employment or promotion of those groups whom he dislikes; he grouches if women are employed in his department; he gives Jewish workers a cold shoulder; he goes on a walk-out in protest against employment of Negroes; he does not like the Chinese workers and suspects them of being Japanese in disguise; he airs any national or social prejudices he happens to have—against the Dagoes, the Hunkies, the Oakies, the communists, the white-collar classes, or the capitalists. The professional pipesetter raises his voice in protest against the college students who have invaded his trade and under pressure learned in four weeks what it took him two years of apprenticeship to master. Some workers are passionately devoted to their unions while others are against them or at least against certain of their activities; some think strikes justifiable and others are as vehemently opposed to them. When one considers the dozens of crosscurrents among the ten thousand workers in a single shipyard, one is surprised that ships do somehow get themselves built. The average laboring man is a "good guy," and he certainly ought to receive a proper compensation for his work. Moreover it is unfortunately true that in normal times he usually has difficulty in getting his employers to pay him what his labor is worth, although his condition has become steadily better if one takes a sufficiently long view of the matter. Within little more than a century the working day has shortened from fourteen hours to eight, with a half-day off on Saturday, and wages have risen from a mere pittance to something a man can live on, even though he does not live as well as he wants to or as well as he should. Many labor groups are, however, not content with this slow evolution, and they want to use the war as a lever to get increases in a hurry. Having belonged for many years to an underpaid profession I can understand the temptation to grasp at any opportunity to better oneself. Perhaps the welders, carpenters, or electricians are equally underpaid; I wouldn't know, but I am quite sure that no group of people has a right to stop work when the country needs them. Their troubles are probably real enough and perhaps critical, but any lowering of the war effort for personal reasons is childish. What good will it do a man to get a raise if he helps lose the war? The average worker undoubtedly believes that Hitler has no business pointing a gun at the heads of innocent people; neither then has he any right to point his most powerful weapon, the strike, at his fellow-countrymen. It certainly does not redound to the credit of coal-miners that they imperiled the war effort four times in six months in order to get a raise for themselves. Nobody begrudges them a reasonable recompense for their work or a raise in pay, but the middle of a long, hard war is no time to be idle. Labor agitators assure the laboring man that this is the psychological moment to hold up the public and get what he is entitled to, and workers are inclined to follow these fanatics all too often.

Because of the concentration of all kinds of people

within relatively small geographical areas where war industries are located, there is constant danger of emotional explosion unless the workers grow up and learn to be tolerant of each other and to submerge their differences for the good of the entire group. In some plants wise leadership by either the owners or responsible workmen has managed to weld together discordant elements into an efficient working force, but in other plants the crosscurrents have been too strong. Strikes and riots have been the outward expression of intolerance and bitter hatreds. Everyone's nerves are understandably on edge from the worries inevitably accompanying war, and antagonisms flare up quickly. Perhaps these outbursts could be more easily prevented or controlled if people recognized them as signs of immaturity rather than of depravity. Presumably the only people who might disapprove completely of collective bargaining by groups of workers are the operators—and they brought it on themselves—but there are times for stopping work and bargaining and times for keeping on the job whether or not one is satisfied. The latter course requires self-control, a characteristic of adulthood. The members of certain unions evidently have it, for they have made no effort to use the national crisis to better themselves, but other groups have followed irresponsible, immature, fanatic demagogues, whose leadership has all the intolerance and selfishness of Hitler's own. In the course of the war, labor may grow up, but thus far it has succeeded only partially in so doing.

Finally, there is the matter of post-war adjustment. To solve the problems involved Americans will need great stability and maturity. After the last war we just came home and washed our hands of the whole business. Perhaps our influence could not have produced a just peace or have made the League of Nations work, but we could have done something more constructive than to stage a typical escape into play on a national scale. For ten years we played merrily and let the world burn if it wanted to. It is to be hoped that at the end of this war we shall have the maturity to face problems instead of running away from them, to follow the path of duty rather than the path of pleasure, to lead the way in mature and responsible thinking, to stand fast in the face of all intolerance, and to insist upon the enactment of a just peace—one that will punish leaders and governments but not the common people who have only done as they were told. I do not mean an easy peace but a just one, in which all nations including our own share in responsibility and blame and punishment. If we can as a nation grow up soon enough, we can be of great assistance in guiding the post-war world in such a way as to prevent another conflagration of the present type. It can be done, however, only by giving security to everyone including the conquered. The peace after our Civil War was the result of such an attitude of the winner toward the loser. By insisting upon tolerance, security, and no retaliation, the breach in the union was healed and we remained a nation. To be sure individual Northerners undoubtedly did show injustice, intolerance, and greed, and individual Southerners were suspicious of Yankees, but the official attitude which continued long after temporary passions had died down stood for reconciliation without punishment. We still have our sectional differences of opinion, but we are in no danger of another civil war; refusal to demand an eye for an eye and a tooth for a tooth mended the break. By comparison the Peace of Versailles was based upon the idea of retribution. Moreover it merely postponed most of the problems which precipitated the first war and increased the insecurity of the German people, with the result that the same forces again came to the surface even though in altered form. I have heard many people say that the trouble with us in 1918 was that we did not march on into Berlin and really finish the war. I doubt that any war was ever won by an army. It is a soldier's business to tear down the old, not to build the new. He can pave the way to victory and that is all he can do. We shall win or lose the present war as a result of what we do after the Germans, Italians, and Japanese have laid down their arms. But to take such a course as is needed to bury the causes of war along with the war dead will require a great deal of maturity.

A vital problem in the world of tomorrow will be the allocation of power. Someone has to have it, and those who have it can misuse it. On the other hand, if properly used it is the greatest force for good in the world. If either complete democracy or complete justice were possible this problem would not be so acute, but in large groups the actual power always has to be delegated to specific individuals. If either the leaders or the citizens of a nation become moved entirely by self-interest they have in their hands the inherent power to wreck a carefully constructed world peace, unless that peace rests upon a potential brute force greater than that of any of its participants separately. This fact will be unpalatable to the idealist, but a peace that disregards the realities of power or does not harness them for constructive use has little chance of survival. At the moment the Allies are firmly united in the effort to gain a victory over their enemies, but it remains to be seen if this alliance can be maintained and broadened so that it may become the foundation for a lasting peace. If each nation wants peace badly enough to surrender some of its sovereignty and to outgrow national self-interest, a workable readjustment can be made; but the treaties upon which the peace rests will have to be written in a spirit of tolerance, unselfishness, and understanding, and they will have to be backed by sheer power so overwhelming that it will not be attacked. The League of Nations has already shown that goodwill alone is not enough, and in recurrent local situations it has been demonstrated that laws must have teeth in order to be effective. Perhaps in some distant future human beings will be adequately motivated by a knowledge of what is just, but until that time a peace that takes present day human reactions into consideration has a better chance for survival than one that is so idealistic as to give encouragement to bad men. Unless the sum total of actual power in the world is directed toward the ends of peace and is so allocated that no one clique can seize it, it will sooner or later produce another war. If all of us are willing to sacrifice for winning the peace just as we are now sacrificing for winning the war, we can have peace, but we shall need more maturity of outlook than some of us have shown thus far.

In our own particular corner of the world, we have one problem that will have to be solved somehow, the problem of our attitude toward and treatment of our citizens of Japanese ancestry. At the moment * most of them are still living, a family to a room, in relocation centers at the far end of nowhere. Anyone who lives on the west coast knows why they had to be removed from circulation—to protect them from our own childishly vindictive Caucasians. Japanese shops were looted, windows were smashed, and Japanese people assaulted on the streets. During blackouts young and old crowded into police and fire stations because those were the only places where they were safe from white hoodlums. The dangers of race riots were so great that all Japanese had to be removed, even those known to be loyal. The F. B. I. knew in advance who most of the dangerous ones were and they were quite competent to discover any whom they had earlier missed without a wholesale removal. In the period from De-

* November 1943.

cember 1941 to May 1942 not one case of sabotage was proved to be the work of Japanese citizens, and in Hawaii they have been officially cleared not only of general charges of sabotage but of responsibility for Pearl Harbor. Their isolation here is therefore due mainly to the immaturity and intolerance of Caucasian majorities in the United States.

Recently I visited one of the relocation centers and talked with many people there. At the moment the authorities are wrestling with the problem of resettling whole families, in the Middle West mostly, and are meeting with the stiffest sort of resistance, although the Japanese are expert farmers and could help relieve the shortage in agricultural workers. The primary difficulty is the unreasoning prejudice of those childish Americans who seem to base their attitudes toward the Japanese upon spy pictures, in which incidentally the villainous rôles are played by our good friends, the Chinese. In some districts the prejudice is so bad that the administration does not dare to send Japanese into them. Yet we have one hundred thirty thousand Japanese, and when the war is over we shall have to do something about them. During the months the Japanese have been living in their remote camps many have developed an attitude of bewilderment, hopelessness, and antagonism, for which they can hardly be blamed. One man put it as follows:

I have been in this country over forty years and I would have become a citizen long ago, only I was not allowed to become one. My children were all born here and my grandchildren. None of us has ever been back to Japan or even wanted to. If we had been content there we should have stayed in the first place. My descendants are American citizens even though I am not. Now comes a war with Japan, and I automatically become an enemy alien, although all my interests are here. I have no life in Japan any longer. My heart is in America where my people are. However if the government had merely put me into this camp I would have forgiven them because after all I am an enemy alien through no fault of my own. But my children were born here; they went to American schools; they belong to American churches; they do not speak Japanese, and the little ones do not even understand it. Why should they be branded as traitors to the only country they know anything about? That white men should be prejudiced against me as a member of another race and another nation is to be understood, but evidently there is no future in America for my descendants either. I came here because I did not like life in Japan and now after forty years of hard work I am robbed of my business and sent into exile. For me life is nearly done, but what will be the attitude of Americans toward my children and grandchildren when the war is over and we are released?

Like all outcasts the Japanese have developed attitudes of resentment and distrust toward those who have discriminated against them, and there are probably more disloyal persons among them now than there were earlier. Another result of our policy of incarceration has recently appeared. When the government asked for volunteers from the camps it got very few. The young men would willingly join the army, in fact many of them indicated their eagerness to do so, but the older men keep restraining them with threats of ostracism for their families. Before the war the Japanese were scattered in little groups of two or three families all over the western states; they were never concentrated in large centers like the Chinese. They were in daily contact with white people and had proved themselves singularly adept at picking up our ways. Their Americanization was progressing rapidly and there was every expectation that within another two or three generations the American born Japanese would cease to be a problem. By throwing them together in camps we have succeeded in blocking the process of Americanization and in giving the forces of Japanization a free hand. The younger generations are now thrown upon the older for company and guidance, not upon their white friends and teachers, and they are in danger of becoming more Japanized day by day. In sharp contrast to the small number of volunteers here was the reaction in Hawaii where the local Japanese have been formally cleared of blame and suspicion, accepted as loyal citizens, and trusted. When the army asked for volunteers it got about three times as many as were requested; these boys are now giving a good account of themselves in the Italian campaign, fighting as well and dying as courageously as any other Americans. No one doubts that there are disloyal Japanese. In all probability they have been supervised too little and allowed too much freedom in winning over others to their point of view. Those known to be disloyal should be kept under supervision for the duration and then if possible sent en masse to Japan. At the best estimates now available there are about fifteen thousand disloyal Japanese. There would therefore be nearly one hundred and fifteen thousand who are harmless, law-abiding Americans. These people have been torn up by the roots through no fault of their own, and they naturally resent it, even though they may admit the necessity. These people cannot justifiably be deported. When the war is over we shall have a difficult problem which is largely of our own creation, and such immature reactions as we have made to date will not solve it.

The entire war situation is, then, not only a return to barbarism but a return to immaturity. The United States is now really getting into the war, but signs of escape into immaturity are still in evidence. The present is certainly the time to grow up, not the time to slide backwards. The unavoidable losses of life and the lowered standards of living will weigh heavily upon everyone, but the burden can be better carried if the average citizen has an adult outlook on life. As a nation Americans have been babied by a high standard of living, by the easy obtaining of comforts, by abundant food, by amusements and sports, by rapid progress in return for honest labor, by the arts of peace, by public education. Many people have found it possible to prolong their immaturity in the absence of strain. Under the new conditions imposed by the war we shall either grow up or crack up. It is to be hoped that eventually we shall develop the mature outlook already shown by the English and Russians, who have been fighting longer, and that we shall learn to welcome such restrictions and privations as have a direct bearing upon a successful prosecution of both war and peace.

If Americans can achieve the necessary maturity they can play an important rôle in determining the nature of the post-war world. But to take our part properly we shall need the intellectual maturity to see our way clearly, the emotional maturity to control ourselves and to face reality with courage, the social maturity to get along tolerantly with people different from ourselves, and the moral maturity to do what we know is right.

Date Due